# Hodder Primary PE

This book is due for return on or before the

# GYMNASTICS

## Patricia Maude

# Hodder & Stoughton

A MEMBER OF THE HODDER HEADLINE GROUP

*British Library Cataloguing in Publication Data*

A Catalogue entry for this title is available from the British Library

ISBN 0 340 65851 7

First published 1997
Impression number    10 9 8 7 6 5 4 3 2 1
Year                 2000 1999 1998 1997

Copyright © 1997 Patricia Maude

Typeset by Fakenham Photosetting Ltd, Fakenham, Norfolk.
Printed in Great Britain for Hodder & Stoughton Educational, a division of Hodder Headline Plc, 339 Euston Road, London NW1 3BH by Scotprint Ltd, Musselburgh, Scotland

# Contents

# Preface

This book is written for teachers, teachers in training, children, parents and governors interested in developing gymnastics in the primary school. It builds from the Programme of Study for Gymnastics in the National Curriculum in Key Stages 1 and 2 (ages 5–11 years), and targets movement vocabulary, skill development, progression, teaching and learning styles and working for quality performance and success. The material is equally useful for those teaching gymnastics outside the National Curriculum.

Aesthetic development through creativity in gymnastics, the promotion of physical activity and the building of healthy lifestyles also feature in the book.

There are also suggestions for planning, teaching, evaluation, assessment, organisation and safety, as well as for updating the school's policy and curriculum document for gymnastics.

The book draws on children's experience, knowledge and understanding of gymnastics through the many photographs of them at work in school.

# Acknowledgements

Inspiration gained from the many children with whom I have worked in schools and at Homerton Gymnastics Club.

The encouragement and support of family and friends.

The staff of Thaxted Primary School and the children whose gymnastics illustrates learning in progress.

Jan Traylen, whose skill and patience have provided the photographs.

# Introduction: child development, the National Curriculum and safety aspects

'*The principle of gymnastics is the education of all youth and not simply that minority of people favoured by nature.*'

(Aristotle, 350 BC)

This book is about gymnastics for all children in primary school in the 21st century! It is about providing opportunities for enhancing the fundamental movement patterns established in infancy, for promoting motor-skill maturity and a physically active and healthy lifestyle in children, and for developing their balance, agility, creative movement expression and skilful performance, through the provision of a challenging and worthwhile gymnastics learning experience.

Gymnastics was one of the core subjects at the time when Aristotle made the statement above. During the Minoan period in Crete, the curriculum included acrobatics, and amongst the early Greeks the two subjects that produced an educated person were gymnastics and music. In this country over the past 100 years, styles of gymnastics have changed markedly and have included military-type training which was followed by Swedish gymnastics and drill, with 'educational gymnastics', inspired by the work of Laban, taking over in the middle of the 20th century. With the arrival of the National Curriculum has come a clarification of both curriculum intention and curriculum content for gymnastics, freeing teachers to develop and deliver a coherent and sequential experience for children throughout their schooling, as part of a broad and balanced programme of physical education.

Children bring with them to school a rich movement vocabulary, emanating from the vast range of experience of moving to learn and learning to move that permeated infancy and the pre-school years. It is both a privilege and a responsibility for the teacher to receive children into Key Stage 1 (ages 5–7 years), to build onto the unique physical and movement development, motor control and play experience of each child, to provide a fulfilling gymnastics education and to send them on to Key Stage 3 (11–14 years of age) as confident, competent and articulate gymnasts.

# ► THE EARLY YEARS

The fundamental movement patterns of early childhood should all be established by the time children start school. *Locomotion* usually started with rolling over and normally proceeded through sitting up, crawling or other forms of creeping, standing up and finally walking. Walking led to toddling, jogging and running, to climbing up and down stairs, as well as to all the play activities that most children will have experienced. However, it is worth remembering several principles of development, particularly on behalf of those children who have developed more slowly and who may need particular help to attain mature patterns of movement.

The first is that of *cephalo-caudal development,* whereby the body develops from the top downwards, with the lower legs and feet being the last to mature. Some children may seem to be clumsy on their feet, and others find it difficult to extend their ankles as they work in gymnastics and need much practice to learn to know what their ankle joints are doing. Full maturity at the 'foot end' of the body may not be attained until Key Stage 2 (ages 7–11 years).

The second of these principles is that of *proximo-distal development* whereby the body develops from the centre outwards, with the functioning of the wrists, hands and fingers being the last to mature. The part played by gymnastics in achieving maturity in the fine functioning of the hand muscles can make a very important contribution to classroom-based work, with its demand for fine finger functioning for writing, painting and cutting, for example. The gross motor functioning required for gymnastics whereby the large muscles are exercised and the large joints develop strength and co-ordination, helps to stimulate the development of the body structure for fine functioning.

A third principle, which affects teaching both in the classroom and in physical education, is the *moment of readiness.* For example, the forward roll depends on the development of the abdominal muscles and the hip flexors to hold the curled position whilst rolling down the spine, and the ability to hop depends both on the muscular strength to fix the pelvis in a horizontal position and on the strength in the ankle muscles to control the body weight over one foot. Another example related to balance is the pace of development of the balance structures in the ears: a slow pace of development here can inhibit the early achievement of fine balance activities, such as bike riding. Finding and using the moment of readiness in teaching and learning gymnastics is a vital clue to successful progression. The design of the syllabus for gymnastics in the National Curriculum gives teacher and learner the opportunity to work with this principle in the achievement of the gymnast's maximum potential.

Finally, the primary school years are the skill-hungry years when children are eager to 'do', to be successful, to learn new skills, and to be agile, co-ordinated, strong, supple and articulate movers. The majority of children enjoy physical activity, provide the teacher with a captive and eager audience, and are ready to work hard and to enjoy their learning.

This book has been planned to provide a base of knowledge about gymnastics, with suggestions for building an effective curriculum for learners and structures for management, teaching and assessment that are attainable for all primary school teachers.

# THE NATIONAL CURRICULUM FRAMEWORK

The National Curriculum provides an excellent framework for the development of a broad, balanced curriculum for all areas of Physical Education and for gymnastics in particular. The statutory content is brief, succinct and comprehensive, and is made up from four separate sections: the Common Requirements, General Requirements, Programme of Study and End of Key Stage Descriptions.

1  *The Common Requirements.* The Common Requirements remind us first that the programme of study should be taught to the great majority of pupils in ways appropriate for their abilities. The implication here is that gymnastics should be inclusive of all children, taking account of their individual needs, abilities and disabilities. Adaptations may be necessary for children with learning difficulties, physical disabilities, or hearing or sight impairment. Second, teaching should take account of providing equal opportunities for boys and girls, and should cater for children from different cultural and language backgrounds. Third, in relation to language, children should be able to express themselves clearly in speech.

2  *The General Requirements.* From the General Requirements, there are a number of important implications for those planning, teaching and assessing gymnastics during Key Stages 1 and 2 (ages 5–11 years):

   ● Pupils should be involved in the continuous process of planning, performing and evaluating, with the greatest emphasis on performing

   ● Pupils should be taught to be physically active, to adopt appropriate posture and use of the body, to engage in activities that develop cardio-vascular health, flexibility, muscular strength and endurance, and to understand the need for personal hygiene

- Pupils should learn to develop positive attitudes, to cope with success and failure, to consolidate performance and to be mindful of others and the environment
- Pupils should learn safe practice, to respond readily to instructions, to recognise and follow relevant rules and safety procedures, to wear appropriate clothing and footwear, to lift, carry and place and use equipment safely and to warm up for and recover appropriately from exercise

3   *The Programme of Study.*
  - Key Stage 1 (ages 5–7 years):
    - Pupils should learn about the changes that happen to their bodies during exercise and should recognise the short-term effects of exercise on the body
    - In gymnastics, they should learn different ways of performing the basic actions of *travelling* using hands and feet, *turning, rolling, jumping, balancing, swinging* and *climbing*, both on the floor and using apparatus
    - They should learn to link a series of actions both on the floor and using apparatus, and be able to repeat these
  - Key Stage 2 (ages 7–11 years):
    - Pupils should learn how to sustain energetic activity over appropriate periods of time, and learn the short-term effects of exercise on the body
    - In gymnastics, they should learn different means of *turning, rolling, swinging, jumping, climbing, balancing* and *travelling* on hands and feet, and how to adapt, practise and refine these actions, both on the floor and using apparatus
    - They should learn to emphasise changes of shape, speed and direction through gymnastic actions
    - They should learn to practise, refine and repeat longer sequences of actions, making increasingly complex movement sequences, both on the floor and using apparatus

4   *The End of Key Stage Descriptions.* These indicate the range of performance that children should be able to achieve at the ages of seven and eleven years, at the end of Key Stages 1 and 2 respectively. If these expectations are built into the curriculum plan throughout the key stage, children can be offered appropriate challenge and teachers can raise their levels of expectation of pupil achievement.
  - Key Stage 1:
    - Pupils should be able to plan and perform simple skills safely, and link actions together
    - They should practise to improve performance and work both alone and with a partner

- They should talk about what they have done and make simple judgements
- They should recognise and describe the effects of exercise on their bodies
- Key Stage 2:
  - Pupils should find solutions to the challenges they encounter
  - They should practise, improve and refine performance, and repeat series of movements with increasing accuracy
  - They should work alone, in pairs and in groups
  - They should make simple judgements about their own and others' performance and use this information effectively to improve the accuracy, quality and variety in their own performance
  - They should sustain energetic activity and demonstrate understanding about what is happening to their bodies during exercise

In the next three chapters, the content of the National Curriculum is analysed, starting with the basic actions and their extensions, including floorwork and apparatus work. The latter part of the book includes suggestions for planning, teaching, evaluation and assessment.

For a breakdown of the Year and age groupings for Key Stages 1 and 2, refer to Appendix II at the end of this book.

# SAFETY IN GYMNASTICS LEARNING AND TEACHING

The General Requirements for Physical Education in the National Curriculum lay considerable stress on ensuring safe practice, and provide curriculum planners with clear guidelines to incorporate this into the School Development Plan, the School Safety Policy and the long-, medium- and short-term plans at each Key Stage. All five elements of the Safe Practice section of the General Requirements contain guidance for safety education in gymnastics, as follows: pupils should be taught:

- to respond readily to instructions
- to recognise and follow relevant etiquette and safety procedures
- about the safety risks of wearing inappropriate clothing, footwear and jewellery, and why particular clothing, footwear and protection are worn for different activities
- how to lift, carry, place and use equipment safely
- to warm up for and recover from exercise

Whilst in the past it was sometimes thought that gymnastics could be hazardous and should only be taught by specialist teachers, National Curriculum Gymnastics, as part of a broad balanced physical education for children, contains a curriculum content appropriate for all abilities of children and is capable of being taught safely by all appropriately trained teachers.

Student teachers should always work in the presence of, and under the direct supervision of, a qualified teacher in order to ensure that they follow the school's curriculum, teach correct techniques and progressions, provide a sound learning environment and learn to plan, teach, assess and evaluate constructively as they develop their professional standards.

Teaching children to manage their own safety and to take account of the safety of others should be clearly in evidence as an integral part of the learning experience for the children. Additionally, teachers must be able to demonstrate risk-management and risk-assessment strategies throughout their gymnastics teaching. These will take account of the following aspects of safe provision:

- about the environment:
  - changing area
  - route to the hall
  - floor – clean and non-slip
  - surrounds – management of protruding items
  - heating, lighting and ventilation

- about the children:
  - stages of motor development, co-ordination, stamina, flexibility and strength
  - stages of skill development
  - spatial awareness with regard to personal and general space
  - body awareness and knowledge of personal potential and limitations
  - health and fitness
  - general learning ability and application to gymnastics
  - self-control in movement and in personal behaviour management
  - able to recognise and use their abilities and to respect their limitations
  - maximum time on task
  - paired and grouped for maximum gymnastics learning opportunities
  - following the school code of practice for safety
  - appropriate clothing
  - bare feet or suitable footwear
  - hairstyle and safe management of any accessories worn
  - learning safe practice in apparatus management (see Figure I.1)

**Figure I.1** *Learning the carrying and management of apparatus in Key Stage 1 (ages 5–7 years)*

- about the session:
  - objectives and assessment criteria shared
  - lesson structure and procedure clear
  - lesson content appropriate for the numbers of children in relation to the size of the hall and the apparatus available
  - warm-up appropriate
  - tasks and feedback differentiated
  - progression and challenge appropriate
  - realistic, attainable targets set
  - noise level facilitating concentration and teacher communication with everyone
  - organisation and management activity appropriate and minimal
  - maximum time on task for children
  - maximum time on physical activity for children
  - safe practice teaching incorporated

- about the apparatus:
  - size, weight, dimensions, stability and condition suitable for the tasks
  - set out around the edges of the hall for ease of access when required
  - school policy adopted for lifting, carrying, placing and setting up
  - apparatus spaced for maximum use
  - mats placed for landings and for inversion activities
  - safety check by children and teacher before use
  - damaged apparatus marked and put out of use
  - annual maintenance and safety certificate obtained

- about the teacher:
  - high expectations of safety awareness and practice
  - following the school policy and routines for safe practice
  - knowledge and understanding of the session content
  - knowledge and understanding of apparatus management and use
  - teacher positioning giving opportunity for observation of all children
  - clothing, footwear, hairstyle and accessories appropriate
  - teaching style, skill expectation and anticipated levels of achievement that are appropriately demanding in relation to the children's experience

- about risk assessment and accident procedure:
  - risk assessment in relation to the space, the apparatus, the children and the curriculum undertaken as part of the whole school policy
  - in the event of an accident, school accident policy and procedure followed and accident form completed as appropriate

The key to success in safe practice in gymnastics is to be found in sound organisation, management, lesson structure and content, and an awareness of safe practices and routines for safety that are agreed upon, taught and learnt.

For further information about safe practice in Physical Education in general and in gymnastics in particular, please refer to *Safe Practice in Physical Education* published by BAALPE in 1995 and thereafter (see Appendix I at the end of this book).

# The gymnastics actions of travel, jump and roll

In this chapter, the three basic actions of *travel*, *jump* and *roll* are explained and analysed. Specific techniques are introduced, ideas for developing the actions are suggested, and ways of extending the children's learning opportunities are outlined.

## TRAVELLING ON HANDS AND FEET

Amongst children's early skill acquisitions, the development of locomotion provides the infant with a whole new world to explore, first by crawling or creeping and then by walking and later running. Refining of those locomotor skills, improving their quality and increasing the child's movement vocabulary of travelling actions is a fundamental part of the gymnastics curriculum at Key Stages 1 and 2 (ages 5–11 years).

To build movement vocabulary, teach the actions shown in Table 1.1 to your class (see page 11). To each of these actions can be added one or more of the dimensions shown in Table 1.2 (see page 11).

Teaching children to travel skilfully and with control is important, particularly during Key Stage 1 (ages 5–7 years), where it is possible to influence and improve the gait and posture. For example, through observation of walking, check that:

- the foot is being fully used, through a heel-to-toe action
- the foot points forwards in the step
- the shoulders are square
- the arms swing in opposition (as the left foot is stepping, the right arm swings forward)

- the posture is upright and tall, with the head held straight
- the weight is being pushed forwards from the hips as the leg swings forward
- the body faces forward
- the whole action is relaxed, rhythmic, streamlined and resilient.

Learning to be resilient or light and springy on the floor or work surface is a key to efficient travelling and provides evidence of quality in movement. Ask the children to listen to their feet, to travel more softly and to reduce the sound until it cannot be heard. In order to achieve such a reduction in sound, they may need to adjust their posture, speed, body tension or size of step. They may also need to consider the sensitivity with which they place the foot or other weight-bearing body part onto the work surface.

Although not mentioned in the Programme of Study for gymnastics, another fundamental skill to teach and reinforce through the gymnastics curriculum is the ability to *stop* effectively, resiliently and at the right moment. Much can be learnt about control of speed through gymnastics, by teaching deceleration as well as acceleration, muscular control, planning and anticipating.

Travelling actions in gymnastics can include other parts of the body, such as:

- on the seat, using the hands and feet to help to travel using a stepping action
- on the front, by fixing the hands on the floor away from the body and using the hands to pull the body along
- on the front, by fixing the hands near to the body and using the hands to push the body along
- on the seat, fixing the feet away from the seat and using the feet to pull the body along
- on the seat, fixing the feet near to the seat and using the feet to push the body along
- on the back, using the feet to pull or push the body along, as above

Pulling and pushing on the floor and on apparatus are important actions and are particularly helpful in contributing to the development of strength in the upper and lower limbs.

## Using the movement vocabulary of travelling

- Travelling should be built into the warm-up, to help develop awareness of personal space within the general space, and as a means of raising the heart rate and getting out of breath.
- Travel should be incorporated into floorwork, particularly when the other actions being practised tend to be static – e.g. balance, travel, balance.

| Travel using feet | Travel using hands and feet |
|---|---|
| Walk | 2 hands and 2 feet, back up |
| Tiptoe | 2 hands and 2 feet, front up |
| Stride | 2 hands and 1 foot, back up |
| Jog | 2 hands and 1 foot, front up |
| Trot | 1 hand and 2 feet, back up |
| Run | 1 hand and 2 feet, front up |
| Gallop | 1 hand and 1 foot |
| Hop along on right foot | 2 hands and 2 feet, turning over |
| Hop along on left foot | Low, stepping around cartwheel |
| Skip (step, hop) | Cartwheel to right and to left |
| Jump (2 feet to 2 feet) | Bunny jump |
| Leap (1 foot to the other) | Walk in handstand |
| Hopscotch (hop to 2 feet, jump to 1 foot) | |
| Chassée (step, join feet, step on same foot) | |
| Chassée-hop (step, join feet, step on same foot and hop) | |

**Table 1.1** *Building movement vocabulary*

| Direction | Body shape | Speed |
|---|---|---|
| Forwards | Long | Slowly |
| Sideways to the right | Short | Accelerating |
| Sideways to the left | Spread out | Quickly |
| Backwards | Tucked in | Decelerating |
| Straight | Flexed/extended hips | Stop |
| Turning | Flexed/extended shoulders | With rhythm |
| Diagonally | Flexed/extended elbows | |
| Circling clockwise | Flexed/extended wrists | |
| Circling anti-clockwise | Flexed/extended knees | |
| Zig-zag | Flexed/extended ankles | |
| Towards | Tall | |
| Away from | | |
| Around | | |
| Under | | |
| Over | | |
| Through | | |
| High | | |
| Low | | |

**Table 1.2** *Developing movement vocabulary*

**Figure 1.1** *Travelling on feet or on hands and feet – working with a partner, leading and following*

**Figure 1.2** *The cartwheel – travelling using hands and feet*

- Travel provides opportunities to move towards, onto, along, off and away from apparatus, and enables children to create dynamic links between floor and apparatus and to incorporate both floor and apparatus into their gymnastics. Travel can also be used to create sequences, or as a link for other actions, and where gymnasts work hard enough to raise their heart rate and get out of breath, travelling can also contribute to cardio-vascular fitness.

## JUMPING AND LANDING

Often referred to as flight, jumping is the ability to defy gravity, to use muscular strength to project the body weight vertically off the floor or apparatus, into the air, using a powerful drive through the feet. This is achieved by co-ordinating the vigorous extension of the ankles, knees and hips from their flexed starting position, to drive the body up from the floor, with a forward and upward swing of the arms to add lift to the jump. Whilst control in the take-off phase is fundamental to the success of the jump, equally important are the co-ordination of the body to sustain control whilst airborne and body tension, resilience and balance in the landing. Teaching all three phases of jumping (the take-off, flight phase and landing), as well as an extensive vocabulary of jumps, are the challenges for the teacher.

As suggested later in the section on rolling, learning the *ending* of complex skills can often hasten the mastery of the whole skill. For the **landing** from jumping to be successful: the legs must flex with strength at the ankles, knees and hips as the balls of the feet touch the ground first, moving through to the whole foot; with the hips kept over the feet and the shoulders over the hips; so that the gymnast, rather than sinking heavily towards the floor, is able to recoil and be springy in standing up by extending at the knees and hips to complete the landing, and by holding the body weight in controlled tension over the feet; with eyes looking forward and arms coming to rest in control at the sides of the body. Apparatus such as benches, low movement tables or stools (preferably between 10 and 25 centimetres in height), each with a mat, provides an ideal environment to practise landing, as the effort of managing the jump phase is not required in this situation and the gymnast can concentrate on the landing and learn to land on two feet with the body weight held over the feet to maintain balance. Using low apparatus helps to ensure that there is not as much pressure through the joints as would be caused by coming down from higher apparatus. It is also easier to get back up onto low apparatus, thereby providing for more turns and therefore more practice and more opportunities for improvement. Check that the take-off is from two feet, to enable children to control the symmetrical, two-footed landing.

To achieve the elevation and control in flight as shown by the gymnasts in Figure 1.3, you might give the following teaching points:

- In the preparation for take-off:
  - flex the ankles, knees and hips
  - swing the arms down and back
  - hold the body with a slight forward lean over the almost flat feet
  - look forward with the eyes

- In the take-off phase:
  - extend the ankles, knees and hips with power as the feet push off the floor, from the heels to the balls of the feet
  - as the ankles extend, swing the arms forward and up to stop beside the eyes to assist the lift of the body and to help maintain the body shape in a straight line rather than in a banana shape
  - keep the shoulders low
  - the eyes continue to look forward to maintain spatial control
  - hold the body in a straight line with tension throughout

Successful jumping and landing demand considerable body awareness, strength and co-ordination, and these may not all be in place for some

**Figure 1.3** *Children aged 5–7 years practising straight jumps and landings*

children, particularly in Early Years (Nursery and Reception) and Key Stage 1 (ages 5–7 years). Cephalo-caudal development may not be complete by the time some children start school, and they may therefore lack the co-ordination and muscular strength required to succeed in taking off to jump from the floor. Some Early Years children are unable to hop as they cannot yet fix the pelvis and transfer the body weight over to one foot and maintain a balance on that foot in order to take off. When learners are ready to hop, they are more likely to move forwards rather than to hop on the spot, at first.

Early attempts at jumping are often first experienced in coming down from very low apparatus, as described on page 13, often leading with one foot before the other, more like stepping off with one foot to land on two feet, rather than taking off from two feet to land on two feet.

Progressions that can help immature jumping to develop and can help to enhance the mature jump further include:

- bouncing:
  - from two feet to two feet, concentrating on resilience and rebound
  - teaching the gymnast to be springy in landing – to treat the floor as glass and to try not to crack it!
  - teaching rebound so that each landing is the start of the next take-off, treating the floor as a hot surface and trying to keep off it! Bouncing on the spot and across the floor can also help to develop muscular strength.

- hopping:
  - along
  - on the spot
  - on one foot and on the other

- practising shapes that will be held during the airborne phase of the jump:
  - in lying, e.g. in a straight (pin) shape on the front, side, back, other side; with arms extended by the eyes, as above: in a star, tucked, or in an asymmetrical shape
  - in standing, e.g. as above, with body tension to hold the shape still
  - in support, e.g. front, back, side supports as in Figure 1.4 (on page 16), with body tension, to hold the body straight

## Extending the vocabulary of jumping and landing

By the end of Key Stage 2 (i.e. by the age of 11), children should have a large vocabulary of known jumps and landings and should be able to categorise these and have them available for sequence work on the floor and using apparatus. The categories might include:

**Figure 1.4** *Practising front and back supports to learn more abut the straight body shape and about tension in the body, to improve jumping*

1   take-offs and landings:
   - from two feet to two feet
   - from two feet to right foot
   - from two feet to left foot
   - from right foot to two feet (as in long jump or vault take-off )
   - from left foot to two feet (again as in long jump or vault take-off )
   - from right foot to right foot (hop)
   - from left foot to left foot (hop)
   - from right foot to left foot (leap)
   - from left foot to right foot (leap)

2   jumps and landings involving other parts of the body:
   - *bunny jump* (see Figure 1.5 opposite)
   - place hands in front of body, flat on the work surface, shoulder-width apart and with fingers pointing forwards, and jump from two feet to two feet on the spot
   - place hands as for the last point, and jump feet together to a new place
   - use apparatus for bunny jumps along, onto and off, or over

**Figure 1.5** *Learning bunny jumps on apparatus in Key Stage 1 (ages 5–7 years)*

3 directions:
- jump forwards
- jump sideways right
- jump sideways left
- jump backwards
- jump diagonally
- jump to make a pathway on the floor or apparatus

4 adding another basic action:
- jump with a quarter turn to the right and to the left
- jump with a half turn to the right and to the left
- jump with a three-quarter, full and more-than-full turn to the right and to the left
- jump into a forward roll (dive roll)

5 body shape in the jump:
- wide arms and legs (star)
- flexed hips and knees (tuck)
- wide legs, flexed hips (straddle)

**Figure 1.6** *Children aged 9–11 years practising jumps with shapes from apparatus*

**Figure 1.7** *A leapfrog over a partner*

**Figure 1.8** *A squat onto a box*

- straight legs, flexed hips (pike)
- one leg forward, one leg back (towards splits)
- asymmetry in arms and legs

Success in jumping and landing leads to some of the most exciting, challenging, satisfying and visually attractive gymnastic experiences and performances, once the gymnast has learnt:

- how to drive powerfully off the floor to gain maximum flight time
- how to co-ordinate the limbs and control body tension to make a clear shape in the air
- how to increase resilience in landing and listen to the feet until they cannot be heard

**Figure 1.9** *A jump into a handstand forward roll on a box*

- how to use the landing to continue or to complete a sequence
- how to use jumping to get onto, off or over apparatus (see Figure 1.6 on page 18), or to jump whilst on top of apparatus
- how to jump onto and from increasingly higher apparatus (see Figure 1.8 on page 19)
- how to use unstable and moving apparatus to achieve more skilful jumping and landing
- how to sequence a series of contrasting jumps
- how to include jumping and landing in sequences of increasing complexity
- how to involve others in partner or group sequences including jumping (see Figure 1.7 on page 18)

# ROLLING

## What is rolling?

*Rolling* is an important core skill in gymnastics and is also a fundamental movement pattern in infants, when they learn to transfer from back to front lying. Children roll before they learn to sit or stand and have had lots of practice at this technique before starting school! They may need to be reminded, however, that rolling should be smooth and continuous, with the body weight being transferred successively from one body surface to the very next adjacent surface, so that joints and bony surfaces are protected from knocking onto the floor or apparatus. Complete rolls should go through 360 degrees, should be resilient and silent, and should show clarity of body shape throughout.

There are two main axes of rotation for rolling in gymnastics. These are the longitudinal axis, for sideways rolling, and the horizontal axis, for forward and backward rolling.

### The longitudinal axis

Imagine a pin which goes in through the feet and comes out through the head, rather like a roasting spit! Rolling sideways is the technique to be practised around this axis. Children can usually roll sideways successfully, to the right and left, with the body, arms and legs extended on the floor (see Figure 1.10 on page 22), whilst also learning and experiencing the technique of rolling as a successive, smooth action. A development of this roll for gymnasts with sufficient strength and body tension is to hold the body in a curved or 'dish' shape on the pelvis and to roll with the arms and legs

**Figure 1.10** *Rolling sideways extended*

**Figure 1.11** *Rolling sideways in a 'dish' shape*

extended and held off the floor (see Figure 1.11 above). Another useful sideways roll is the *circle roll* which starts and ends in a sitting position with wide, extended legs (see Figure 1.12 below). Sideways rolls can also be practised in a tucked shape, starting and ending on the knees (see Figure 1.13 below).

**Figure 1.12** *The circle roll*

**Figure 1.13** *Rolling sideways tucked*

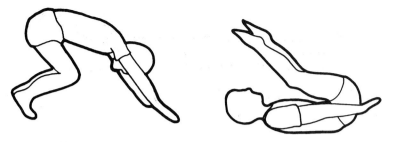

**Figure 1.14** *Rolling around the horizontal axis*

### The horizontal axis

Imagine a pin going through a gymnast's waist from side to side. Rolling forwards and backwards are the two directions of rolling around this axis (see Figure 1.14 above).

## Building a vocabulary of rolls

The main challenges for children are to build up a large movement vocabulary of separate rolls, to refine the body shape in each and to develop the essential qualities of continuity, resilience and successive flow of movement over adjacent body parts. Table 1.3 on page 24 gives some suggestions for building a vocabulary of rolls, categorised according to the

**Figure 1.15** *Practising rolling along the floor*

| | Axis of rotation | |
|---|---|---|
| | *Longitudinal* | *Horizontal* |
| *Direction* | Sideways to the right | Forwards |
| | Sideways to the left | Backwards |
| *Body shape* | Extended on whole body | Tucked (squat) |
| | Extended, dish shape, on pelvis | Extended knees and ankles during roll |
| | Tucked (kneeling start) | Straddle (wide legs) |
| | Straddle, on seat with wide legs (circle roll sideways) | Twisted, over one shoulder |
| | 1 knee flexed, other extended | |
| | Alternate flexion and extension of legs and arms during roll | |
| *Start and end positions* | On back | Feet together |
| | On front | Feet apart, with wide legs |
| | On knees | On knees into forward roll |
| | On seat | On seat into backward roll |
| | On 1 knee and other foot | On 1 foot |

**Table 1.3** *Building a vocabulary of rolls*

axis of rotation, the direction of travel, the body shape of the roll and the part of the body used as the base for the starting and finishing positions.

Progression in the teaching of rolling will take account of the child's previous experience and current stage of development in terms of body shape, size, strength, flexibility, co-ordination, spatial awareness and courage. Experience should include rolling along mats, along the floor (see Figure 1.15 on page 23) and onto, along and from apparatus. To increase the movement vocabulary and to add to the complexity and challenge of the work, teach a variety of starting or finishing positions. Rolls can also incorporate changes in body shape and changes in the extension and flexion of the legs or arms during the roll. Additionally, similar or contrasting rolls can be joined into sequences, and rolls can be included in sequences with other actions both on the floor and using apparatus.

## Teaching the Forward and Backward Rolls

For many children, the *forward roll* and the *backward roll* are complex skills to achieve on the floor and are often more easily learnt down inclined apparatus with a soft surface (see Figure 1.16 opposite). Forward rolls can also be learnt

**Figure 1.16** *(a) Forward roll down a ramp, (b) backward roll down a ramp. Here, the softness of the apparatus protects the head and small bones of the spine, the cuboid provides a flat starting platform, and the incline of the ramp provides the momentum to enable the gymnast to push the body over the head*

from a low platform onto a mat on the floor. Once gymnasts are familiar with the concept of rolling and are experienced at rolling sideways, they are more likely to succeed with the forward and backward rolls.

When learning the forward roll, it can be helpful to teach the ending before the beginning. Rocking and standing up is the last part of the forward roll. Teach children to rock down the spine from the shoulders to the seat, in a tucked shape, to place the feet on the mat near to the seat and, with the arms and hands reaching forwards, to transfer the weight to the feet to stand up. Children can help each other to achieve this by taking hold of each other's hands to assist the standing-up phase of the ending. These practices help to establish body awareness, spatial knowledge and orientation, and can provide the confidence to enable the more reluctant gymnast to tackle the first part of the action. However, some young children may not have developed the musculature to retain the tucked shape and may need to hold the knees when rocking.

### The technique of the forward roll

The technique of the forward roll in a tucked shape involves the following actions:

- From standing, flex the hips and knees to lower into a squat position on the feet
- Place the hands flat on the mat with fingers pointing forwards
- Check that the hands are placed shoulder-width apart and well forward in front of the body
- Raise the hips by extending the knees to transfer the weight to the hands
- Flex the neck to tuck the head in, bringing the chin nearer to the chest

**Figure 1.17** *Starting the forward roll with wide legs lowers the body, making it easier to transfer the weight onto the hands and shoulders and also helps to avoid knocking the nose on the knees!*

- Push with control from the feet, to extend the ankles, keeping the knees extended
- Lower the shoulders by flexing the elbows slowly to place the shoulders onto the mat, as near to the hands as is comfortable. The arms should work with strength to achieve this controlled lowering of the shoulders
- Rock smoothly down the spine from the shoulders to the seat
- Flex the knees and ankles, to place the feet near the seat on the mat
- Transfer the weight to the feet
- Reach forwards with the arms and hands to stand up

Once the roll is confidently performed in the tucked shape, the gymnast can learn to extend the knees and ankles to show straight legs both as the shoulders are placed on the mat and during the rolling phase and can then flex them again to transfer the weight to the feet to stand up.

**Figure 1.18** *Another progression to help develop the forward roll is to roll from apparatus onto a mat. Here, the gymnast learns to take the weight on the hands and uses the strength of the arms to flex the elbows and to lower the shoulders onto the mat with control, to complete the roll*

## The technique of the backward roll

The technique of the backward roll in a tucked shape involves the following actions:

- From standing, flex the hips and knees to lower into a squat position on the feet
- Lower to sitting, and continue to roll from the hips, up the spine, to the shoulders

**Figure 1.19** *A further progression for the forward and backward rolls, before proceeding to a mat on the floor, is to use a springboard covered with a mat, as the slight incline provides sufficient momentum to enable the gymnast to complete the roll*

- Flex the elbows to place the hands flat on the mat, beside the ears, with the fingers pointing towards the seat and the elbows above the ears, ready to push, to extend the elbows with strength
- Use the momentum of the rolling action, and time the strong extension of the elbows to make space to push the body over the head, thus avoiding putting pressure on the neck
- Place the feet on the mat and continue to push with the hands, extending the arms to lift the body to stand up

Developing the strength and timing to extend the elbows at exactly the right moment, to make space between the arms large enough for the head to go through, is a great achievement for the learner.

Rather than helping gymnasts by supporting them at the hips and lifting them over onto their feet, the provision of a comfortable ramp enables them to accomplish the roll unaided and also to take responsibility for their own learning (See Figure 1.16 on page 25).

Once learnt, knowledge of both the forward and backward roll should be extended, by using apparatus, by learning a variety of body shapes, by building

**Figure 1.20** *As with the forward rolls, learning the backward roll with wide legs (straddle), whereby the weight of the legs does not pass directly over the head, is a useful progression towards learning the backward roll to squat*

sequences of rolling, by creating sequences incorporating rolling with other actions and by teaching more complex skills such as handstand into forward roll and backward roll into bunny jump or handstand. Some children may have learnt *dive forward rolls* or *somersaults* (jump, rotate backwards or forwards in the air and land on the feet) in extra-curricular gymnastics sessions. However, unless the teacher is confident that these can be incorporated safely into curriculum sessions, they should not be included.

## Developing rolling using apparatus

In addition to the use of apparatus inclines to provide comfort, momentum and progressions in the learning of forward and backward rolls, placing apparatus in the floor area introduces a range of challenges and provides an ideal environment for the building of an extensive movement vocabulary of rolls. Teach children to roll towards, onto, along and from as many of the apparatus types as are available and suitable in the hall.

Children could build up a record and keep a vocabulary list of the apparatus and the types of rolls learnt:

- low inclined-down and soft-surfaced apparatus, such as *foam wedge* or *springboard* covered with a mat
- higher inclines, such as an *inclined padded bench*
- horizontal, low, wide, soft surfaces such as *foam cuboids, foam box, box top, padded bench platform, movement table*
- horizontal, higher or narrower or harder-surfaced apparatus such as *whole box, bench*
- inclined-up apparatus such as *foam wedge,* inclined *padded bench*

Other apparatus which enable a rolling sensation to be achieved through circling, include:

**Figure 1.21** *Practising forward and backward rolls*

- *ropes*, for circling between two ropes backwards and forwards (see Figure 2.13 on page 46)
- *horizontal pole*, to grip with hands hip-width apart, for circling forwards and backwards (see Figure 2.12 on page 45).
- a *frame* with horizontal bars or poles, as above

## Developing rolling using sequence work

Table 1.4 shows some examples of sequences for children to try:

| Sequence | Examples |
| --- | --- |
| Link two rolls into a sequence | Sideways rolls, extended, then tucked<br>Forward roll to sit in straddle, circle roll sideways |
| Link a roll plus another action into a sequence | Bunny jump, backward roll<br>Balance on one foot, forward roll, gallop |
| Make a new skill | From handstand, roll down forwards to stand |
| Move between levels | Jump from floor to forward roll along a box top, or jump up to roll on whole box |
| Move between levels | Roll forwards to the feet and jump high<br>Roll backwards down a ramp |
| Roll to travel in a sequence | From a balance, roll to travel to a new balance<br>Roll towards apparatus |
| Conclude the landing of a sequence | Jump from apparatus, to land low on feet, then roll to stand |
| Leave apparatus during sequence | From front lying on apparatus, place hands on mat and roll forward onto mat |
| Move into a pairs balance | Tucked sideways roll towards partner, shoulder balance with feet touching |
| Leave a pairs balance | From front support on partner's knees and hands, forward roll to land |

**Table 1.4** *Sequences involving rolls*

Rolling can readily be planned into the curriculum throughout the primary school to ensure that by the beginning of secondary education, children are both confident and competent in the performance of this basic action on the floor, using apparatus, working alone and with a partner.

# The gymnastics actions of balance, turn, twist, swing and climb

The three actions of *balance, turn* and *twist* can be developed both on the floor and on apparatus, whereas *swing* and *climb* are only possible on apparatus. In this chapter, each of these five actions is analysed, and movement vocabulary suitable for children in both Key Stage 1 and 2 (ages 5–7 and 7–11) is introduced.

## ► BALANCING

Achieving sufficient control to stop moving and to hold a balance with a clear shape can be a major challenge, requiring great concentration, particularly for young children who are still developing their gross motor functioning and for growing children whose body is changing shape and size and is making new demands in movement. In gymnastics, there is much to be taught through the topic of balance, to help children to develop sound body knowledge and body management, co-ordination and control, both in stillness and in movement.

An effective curriculum around the topic of balance should include the teaching of:

1  *body awareness* –  knowledge of the body, the relationship of the limbs in balances and the shape of the body in action;

2  *co-ordination* –  the integration of all parts of the body in static positions and when moving;

**3** *body tension –*    the exact amount of muscle strength needed around each joint of the body to achieve control;

**4** *bases –*    the foundations for controlled balances; the part or parts of the body in contact with the work surface, over which the rest of the body is poised;

**5** *centre of gravity –* the point for achieving balance over the selected base.

Let us consider each of these in more detail:

# 1 Body awareness

Knowledge of the body and of the relationship of the limbs as they work is fundamental to understanding the body in action. Young children should be taught to name the parts of their body in action and to describe the skills they are learning in terms of the way the body is working.

Being able to name *parts of the body* as they work is a great achievement for some children:

'I'm balancing on *two hands* and *two feet*', 'I'm balancing on my *back.*' Along with this ability to name body parts in action, they can go on to describe the *shape* of the body: 'My arms are in a *wide* shape and my legs are *straight and together.*'

**Figure 2.1** *'We can balance on our hands'*

**Figure 2.2** *'My body is in a big shape'*

## 2 Co-ordination

Knowing what each joint is doing and where each part of the body is, in relation to all other parts, during a balance and when moving, requires quite sophisticated body and movement knowledge, but is well within the capability of even quite young children. Many children know and can describe what the joints are *doing* as they balance: 'My elbows are *straight*', 'My knees are *bent*.' They can also describe the *relationship* of various body parts: 'My hands are *near to* my feet', 'My back is *far away from* my hands and feet.'

Further description of positioning to aid with co-ordination could include the *levels* of the various parts of the body: 'In this headstand, my head and hands are *low* and my *feet* are high.'

## 3 Body tension

This technical term can be interpreted to help children to understand how much or how little muscle strength is required and the amount of energy that needs to be used to achieve a successful balance with the least amount of effort. Achieving economy and efficiency in movement is a major target!

# 4 and 5 Bases and centre of gravity

When teaching balance, the *base* is that part or parts of the body in contact with the floor or apparatus surface and supporting the rest of the body. The concept of the *centre of gravity* involves positioning the body above and within the base in order to maintain the selected position with control and to avoid wobbling or falling over. It is also important to know how far to shift the centre of gravity to move out of a balance and to move into off-balance situations when needed.

Categorising balances according to the base can provide gymnasts with a framework from which to build a large vocabulary of gymnastic balances and to learn more about the theoretical aspects of balancing. For example, balancing on a large base such as the back, with much of the body in contact with the floor or apparatus, provides greater stability and is therefore easier to hold still than balancing on a small base such as one knee. Examples of categories of base that can provide for greater ease (basic balances) and more difficulty (contrasting balances) are shown in Table 2.1 on page 36.

Helping children to understand the conditions for achieving basic and contrasting balances can provide them with learning structures to become independent in building their own vocabulary of balances, in determining their own progression from easier to more difficult balances and in learning to provide themselves with appropriate levels of challenge.

**Figure 2.3** *Infants learning about bases and body shape*

| Basic balances | Contrasting balances |
| --- | --- |
| Large amount of the body as base | Small amount of the body as base |
| Many body parts as base | Few body parts as base |
| Bases which balance the body the right way up | Bases which balance the body upside down |
| Balances with the body held low and close to the base | Balances with the body held high and far from the base |
| Balances with the body held directly above the base | Balances with the body leaning away from the base |

**Table 2.1** *Examples of bases for basic and contrasting balances*

**Figure 2.4** *Balances using floor and apparatus*

Table 2.2 opposite shows some examples of balances categorised as shown in Table 2.1. These could be used as the basis for developing a class vocabulary of bases, as a guide for moving from easier to more difficult work, or as a stimulus for the development of *sequences*.

## The development of balance

When planning units of work on the theme of balance, it is important to include some vigorous activities to contrast with the inevitably rather static

**Examples of bases for basic balances**

| | | *The right way up* | *Body held low to the base* | *Body held directly over the base* |
|---|---|---|---|---|
| *Large base* | *Many body parts as base* | | | |
| Front | 2 feet, 2 hands and head | Sitting | On feet, crouched down | 2 hands and 2 feet, seat up |
| Back | Seat, 2 hands and 2 feet | Kneeling up | On back, tucked | Standing |
| Side, legs spread out | 2 hands and 2 feet | Standing | Kneeling down low | 2 hands and 2 feet, front up |

**Examples of bases for contrasting balances**

| | | *Upside-down* | *Body held high from the base* | *Body leaning away from the base* |
|---|---|---|---|---|
| *Small base* | *Few body parts as base* | | | |
| Hip | 1 foot | On shoulders | Extended shoulder balance | 2 hands and 1 foot, body outside base |
| Foot | 2 hands | Headstand | Handstand | 1 hand and 1 foot, body outside base |
| Seat | 1 hand and 1 foot | Bunny jump | Arabesque | On seat, leaning back |

**Table 2.2** *Building a vocabulary of balances*

**Figure 2.5** *Balances with body held low to or high from the base*

work and sometimes limited work rate generated by practising balances. To provide relief, too, from the demanding level of concentration that balance requires, tasks could be set which:

- involve travelling to a new space between each balance
- require the gymnast to link other actions to balances
- encourage gymnasts to learn a range of movements that lead into balances, as well as movements that take the gymnast out of balances
- ensure that gymnasts gain experience on the full range of apparatus available

Teaching a gymnastics unit on the theme of balance, by means of *task cards*, can help children to plan, perform, evaluate and assess their gymnastics, and can extend their ability to become independent learners. Such a theme would be particularly suitable for children whose preferred learning style is one of self-guided study, and a real challenge for children who are normally teacher-dependent. The role of the teacher here would be to:

- ensure that the children have understood the tasks
- provide feedback to increase the level of content
- give feedback to enhance the quality of performance
- encourage a high work rate
- assist gymnasts in assessment
- monitor and maintain safety and the organisation of the whole class

Suggested instructions for task cards are as follows:

- Practise and record one balance from each category of contrasting balances that you can show on low apparatus
- Practise and record one balance from each category of basic balances that you can show on higher apparatus
- Practise and record three balances that are partly on the floor and partly on apparatus, and that are challenging for you
- Practise, and link by travelling, two contrasting balances on apparatus that show symmetry, and record the sequence

**Figure 2.6** *Symmetrical shapes on apparatus*

- Practise, and link by jumping, two contrasting balances on the floor that show asymmetry, and record your sequence
- Observe the performance of another gymnast, and give feedback to help improve performance
- Practise and record three balances that show excellent body tension, on the floor
- Practise and record three balances that show excellent extension, on apparatus
- Practise and list six entries into balances
- Practise and list six exits from balances
- Practise and show a sequence of three balances with a clear starting position, clear links into and from each balance, and a clear finishing position, on floor or apparatus

- Learn two new balances on the floor and record them
- Learn two new balances on apparatus and record them
- With a partner, practise and perform a mirror sequence of three balances, facing each other
- With a partner, practise and perform a sequence of two balances side by side, linked by travelling on the floor

Probably the most difficult balance to be achieved in primary school gymnastics is the *handstand* (see Figure 2.7 below), and for children who can already hold a handstand balance there is still the one-handed handstand to

**Figure 2.7**  *The handstand balance*

learn! Progressions, or activities to practise that can together lead to the successful performance of handstands, should be incorporated widely into the gymnastics curriculum. Such activities can be categorised to provide opportunities for learning:

1  the shape of the handstand:
   - lying in a straight shape
     – on the back
     – on the front
     – on the right side
     – on the left side
   - standing on flat feet in the shape of a handstand, with arms by ears, shoulder-width apart
   - standing on the balls of the feet in the shape of a handstand

2  body tension to adopt in the handstand balance:
   - front support (hands shoulder-width apart, straight line from head to foot, as seen in Figure 2.8)
   - back support (see Figure 2.8)

**Figure 2.8** *Front support and back support*

   - side support on the right side
   - side support on the left side
   - supports part on apparatus, part on floor

3  spatial awareness in the inverted position:
   - balance on two hands and two feet, seeing the world upside-down
   - balance on two hands and one foot
   - shoulder balance(see Figure 2.9 on page 42)
   - headstand with tucked and with extended legs (see Figure 2.9)
   - bunny jump
   - cartwheel
   - forward and backward rolls

**Figure 2.9** *Practising the shoulder balance and headstand*

Competent performance of the above activities can provide the gymnast with sufficient knowledge and confidence to achieve successful handstands, once the entry into and the exit from the handstand have been taught.

To go into handstand from standing up, the gymnast needs to take a long step with one foot and go through a lunge shape, keeping the body as straight as possible and pushing the flexed knee forward over the foot as the hands reach for the floor (see Figure 2.10 opposite), so that the leading leg can swing up with an extended knee and ankle, straight to the vertical position above the hands, whilst the lunging foot pushes off the floor, the knee straightens and the leg swings up straight to join the leading leg.

To land, the legs lower with control, one after the other, so that the feet return with control to the mat or floor, one after the other, and the hands push off the floor to help to lift the chest back up to a standing position.

Once learnt, the handstand can be practised on apparatus of increasing height and decreasing dimension, and other skills can be added to it such as the forward roll (from handstand balance, flex the elbows slowly to lower the shoulders to the mat into the roll), or the backward roll to handstand, or headstand into handstand.

Gymnasts who can achieve this level of control and management of

**Figure 2.10** *The lunge shape*

handstands can be encouraged to develop further progressions, such as turning in handstand, or working on other apparatus (see Figures 1.9 and 2.11).

**Figure 2.11** *A handstand with forward roll on apparatus*

# TURNING

*Turning* involves the change of direction of the whole body, as a single unit, as in jumping up and making a half-turn in the air, to land facing in the opposite direction, or as in lying on the floor and rolling over from back to front to back, or as in performing a cartwheel or a forward roll.

The three main axes for rotation in gymnastics are:

**1** *the longitudinal or head-to-foot axis.* Imagine a pin going in through the top of the head and out through the feet (or seat) as an axis about which the gymnast can rotate.

Some activities that use this axis for turning are:

● rolling, sideways, tucked or extended

● jumping, to turn to the right and to the left for an eighth, quarter, half or three-quarter turn or more

● spinning, on one foot or on the seat, for part or whole turns or more

● stepping, to turn around on the feet, on the hands, or on the hands and feet, when turning over from front support to back support

● hanging on a rope as it untwists

**2** *the horizontal or side-to-side axis.* Imagine a pin going in through one side of the body and out through the other as an axis around which the gymnast can rotate.

Some activities that use this axis are:

● rocking on the back

● rolling forwards and backwards

● circling around a pole, forwards and backwards (see Figure 2.12 opposite)

● circling between two ropes, forwards and backwards (see Figure 2.13 on page 46)

**3** *the dorsi-ventral or front-to-back axis.* Imagine a pin going in through the stomach and out through the back.

Some activities that use this axis for turning are:

● cartwheel to the right and to the left (see Figure 2.14 on page 46)

● spin on the front or on the back

Turning enables a gymnast to change direction, and when used as a link, can add variety and complexity to actions and sequences.

**Figure 2.12** *Circling around a pole*

**Figure 2.13** *Circling between two ropes*

**Figure 2.14** *Cartwheel*

# TWISTING

Another action which is similar to the turn and which is also useful both to change direction and to use as a link is the *twist*. Although this action is not contained in the Programme of Study until Key Stage 3 (11–14 years of age), a basic knowledge of how it differs from the turn will prevent later confusion.

When twisting, the gymnast fixes one part of the body or keeps it facing in the original direction, changes direction with the rest of the body and then completes the rotation of the action. Three examples of twisting are:

1   from balancing on the knees, twist at the waist to lower the hips and raise the knees into a balance on the seat;

2   from shoulder balance, twist in the spine, to take the knees over one shoulder to a knee balance;

3   bunny jump over a bench, taking off from one side and twisting at the waist to land on the other side.

Helping children to distinguish turn from twist will not only enhance and enrich their movement vocabulary, but will also enable them to be increasingly more analytical in their gymnastics.

# SWINGING AND CLIMBING

These two basic actions of *swinging* and *climbing* can be considered together, since, unlike all the other basic actions, they cannot be practised on the floor and can only be learnt where appropriate apparatus is available. Both these actions depend on the gymnast's ability to grip the apparatus so as to provide for themselves a fixed point for initiating the movement of the rest of the body. These two actions are important for teaching safe methds of *gripping* apparatus and for developing strength in the upper body, and they also offer opportunities to explore the environment above the floor. Ideally, the apparatus in the school hall will include ropes, a large frame, trestles, poles, planks, ladders and stools, all of which can be used for hanging, swinging and climbing.

## Hanging and swinging

Much can be learnt about gripping and *hanging* before gymnasts are ready to swing. This experience can be gained from providing a range of apparatus such as horizontal and inclined poles, planks and ladders and vertical apparatus such as ropes, poles and frames (see Figure 2.15 on page 48). Children can then be taught to hang from the hands and feet, from the front of the hips, from the backs of the knees and from under the shoulders, as well as from the hands alone, when the hands, arms and shoulders are strong enough to manage the suspended weight of the whole body. Children should learn to hang the right way up as well as upside-down (see Figure 2.16 opposite) and at all times to land safely and quietly. Quiet landings depend on muscular strength to hold the body as well as body and spatial awareness to place the feet resiliently onto the floor.

Once they have gained sufficient strength, in the hands to grip, and in the upper part of the body to hang, gymnasts should practise hanging from a rope with the body weight suspended from the hands, before proceeding to the swing. Swinging involves taking the rope away from the vertical and jumping up to grip the rope with the hands or with the hands and feet, to let the rope swing to and fro (see Figure 2.17 opposite). Again, the landing must be safe and controlled, so it is best to try short, low swings first and progress to longer and higher swings. Swinging can also be experienced, for example, from hanging with hands and feet under a horizontal pole. More experienced gymnasts may be ready to learn to swing onto and from other pieces of apparatus, demonstrating their high level of skill in taking off, swinging and landing safely.

**Figure 2.15** *Hanging on the frame*

**Figure 2.16** *Hanging upside-down on the frame*

**Figure 2.17** *Swinging on ropes and rope ladder*

# Climbing

Most children will have had much experience of climbing in the home and on playgrounds before they come to school, so it is important to build on that experience with regular and frequent opportunities to use the school apparatus for climbing, from the earliest gymnastics lessons onwards. Climbing helps to develop co-ordination and is an important activity for helping to develop strength in the upper part of the body. The large frame offers an ideal environment for climbing up, along, through, diagonally and down, as does other apparatus such as trestles or high stools.

**Figure 2.18** *Climbing and hanging on ropes and rope ladder*

Rope climbing (see Figure 2.18 opposite) is an aspiration of most children, and is tantalisingly difficult for those whose ratio of weight to strength does not permit then to defy gravity and pull themselves up! If strength does permit, then the action here is one of alternately gripping and pulling up with the hands and pushing up with the feet, so that the body transfers alternately from an extended shape to a small shape. To come down, gymnasts must remember to keep the upper legs wide, to prevent the rope rubbing the skin and causing a burn, and to maintain a strong grip with the hands and the feet to control the descent. They must also learn to start the downward climb before getting tired, as the pull of gravity in the descent demands almost as much energy as when working against gravity in the ascent!

Children should expect to gain in strength, agility, speed and security as they gain in climbing experience. However, once they reach puberty, the change in body shape and size may make rope climbing more difficult for some children unless they maintain and continue to develop their upper body strength.

# Gymnastics development into Key Stage 2 and towards Key Stage 3

As soon as children in Key Stage 1 (ages 5–7 years) have a working knowledge of some of the basic actions of gymnastics and have established a performance vocabulary of those actions, they are ready for one or more of the following challenges:

1  *to perform those basic actions with better technique, to improve their quality.* This might require more knowledge about the actions themselves, or may be dependent on better co-ordination, greater muscular strength, improved flexibility, increased body tension and more power or fluency, accuracy, economy, control or precision in movement, all of which can be developed over time as the gymnast grows, matures, practises and gains experience. The role of the teacher is crucial in this regard, for it is the teacher who can observe the moment when the child is physically, mentally and educationally ready to proceed to the next stage. It is also the teacher who can help the children to recognise the moment of readiness for themselves.

2  *to link basic actions into sequences and to develop movement memory.* This will require the gymnast not only to have knowledge and experience of the actions to be linked, but also to develop the memory to be able to perform the first action whilst anticipating the second action, including appropriate linking movements when necessary. The teacher's role is to teach the children to follow one action with another, to teach a wide vocabulary of linking movements to be drawn from in building sequences, and to enable children to find appropriate solutions to the challenges set by the task. For example:

- the direct link of step and hop enables the child to build up the *skipping* action, the direct link between hop and jump facilitates the *hopscotch* action, and the direct link between step and jump to two feet leads to the accurate use of a springboard for *vaulting* and also to the take-off and landing in the *long jump*

- the link of *bunny jump* to *sideways roll* requires movement to get from the feet landing of the bunny jump into the side, back or front lying position to start the roll. The vocabulary of appropriate linking movements might include:

  - from landing on the feet, transfer weight backwards to sit down and lie down on the back, extending the arms and legs ready for the roll
  - keep tucked when landing from the bunny jump, place knees on mat and slide hands forward to lie on the front
  - from tucked landing, place knees and lower body onto side, to extend in lying on the side

- to link a *cartwheel* and a *shoulder balance*, the gymnast must first decide whether to select the gravity-assisted sequence of starting with the cartwheel and lowering into the shoulder balance, or whether to work against gravity by starting with the shoulder balance. Then, how many appropriate links are there to develop the range and quality of the gymnast's movement vocabulary and to teach the gymnast to be efficient in movement?

3 *to develop a vocabulary of body shapes for gymnastics*. Precision in gymnastics performance is challenging, especially for children in Key Stage 1. Helping children to develop body awareness, to know the position of the limbs in relation to each other and to the whole body, and to focus on clarity of body shape is a central focus of Key Stage 1 teaching, towards achieving that precision.

The three basic symmetrical body shapes in gymnastics are:

- *small*, tucked, folded, with all joints flexed
- *straight*, long, extended, with all joints stretched (including ankles, knees, hips, spine, shoulders, elbows, wrists and fingers), with arms extended near the ears and shoulder-width apart, and with the legs together, knees and ankles near to each other
- *wide*, star-shaped, symmetrical, with ankles, knees, hips, spine, shoulders, elbows, wrists and fingers extended, with feet pushed far from each other and hands also reaching far away from each other

Children will be more likely to be successful in performing these body shapes accurately when they are:

- balancing
- the right way up

- in a stable position
- standing, sitting or lying on the front, back or side, as appropriate
- able to see the location of their arms and legs
- able to observe the extension/flexion of their joints
- copying someone else showing the shape

Control and accuracy of body shape is usually more difficult to achieve when they are:

- unable to see the joints and the location of the arms and legs
- balancing on less stable or more difficult bases
- jumping and trying to show the shape whilst in the air, whilst also preparing to land
- inverted, upside-down, managing the unusual orientation

Recording learning using a chart (see Figure 3.1 on page 56) can help children to evaluate their gymnastics knowledge and achievement in relation both to body shape (small, straight or wide) and to orientation, when balancing the right way up, when in the air in a jump and when upside-down. (A blank copy of Figure 3.1 is reproduced in Appendix III as Figure A.1 for teachers to use.)

Further progression in learning about controlled body shape in gymnastics can include categorising shapes according to their *symmetry* (where both sides of the body are the same):

- star shape, straight shape, small shape

or according to their *asymmetry* (where the right side does not look the same as the left side):

- balancing on one foot, one arm high, the other low
- leaping from one foot to the other with one arm forward and the other to the side
- shoulder balance, with twist at waist, with one leg bent and the other straight

4 *to develop spatial dimensions of gymnastics.* Adding to the quality of the basic actions can be achieved by learning more about *directions, pathways* and *levels* and then incorporating these into sequence work: see Table 3.1 opposite.

5 *to develop time elements in gymnastics.* For young children, learning to stop can be quite a challenge, as can control of fast speed. Competent gymnasts should be able to work at slow and fast speeds, as well as learning to accelerate, decelerate and to pause or stop, to develop rhythm in their work and to show several aspects of speed within a single sequence. Dimensions of time are as follows:

- slow
- quick
- accelerate
- decelerate
- pause
- stop

**6**   *to develop relationships with other gymnasts and with the environment.* Once gymnasts can work safely alone, managing their own personal space in the context of the general space shared with others in the class, they can learn to work alongside or with others, both on the floor and when using apparatus – see Table 3.2 below.

| Directions | Pathways | Levels |
| --- | --- | --- |
| Forwards | Straight | High |
| Sideways right | Curved | Medium |
| Sideways left | Zig-zag | Low |
| Backwards | Across | Up |
| Turning | Around | Down |
| | Over | |
| | Under | |
| | Through | |

**Table 3.1** *Spatial dimensions in gymnastics*

| Relationships | Environment |
| --- | --- |
| Alone | On the floor |
| Observing a partner | Onto apparatus |
| Working beside a partner | Off apparatus |
| Leading a partner | On apparatus |
| Following a partner | Along apparatus |
| Mirroring a partner | Towards apparatus |
| Meeting a partner | Under apparatus |
| Parting from a partner | Over apparatus |
| Surrounding a partner | Through apparatus |
| In a group | Around apparatus |

**Table 3.2** *Different kinds of relationship and environment in gymnastics*

This material, when considered alongside that in the next section, can provide a comprehensive framework of gymnastics actions and applications, from which to build the gymnastics curriculum for primary-school children.

|  | Balancing | Jumping | Inverting |
|---|---|---|---|
| Small<br>Flexed<br>Tucked |  |  | hands and feet<br>bunny jump<br>headstand |
| Straight<br>Long<br>Extended |  | from 2 feet to 2 feet<br>stretched jump,<br>arms by ears,<br>ankles, knees and<br>hips extended |  |
| Wide<br>Star | on front<br>on side<br>on back<br>on seat<br>on feet<br>on 2 feet and 2 hands |  |  |

Draw or list your work in the boxes

**Figure 3.1** *A chart for recording body shapes*

# EXTENDING AND DEVELOPING THE GYMNASTICS MOVEMENT VOCABULARY

Once children have successfully attained the End of Key Stage Descriptions for Key Stage 1 (ages 5–7 years), they will be looking for new challenges, further skill acquisition, knowledge and understanding of gymnastics as they mature through to the end of primary school. Maintenance of the basic actions in the Programme of Study will require regular practice and adaptation as children grow, changing in size, shape, strength, speed, endurance and flexibility, and as they accommodate to new lever lengths in the limbs. Also, as children develop greater awareness of all aspects of gymnastics through enhanced observational skill and cognitive ability, so their planning, performance and evaluation of gymnastics should increase in complexity. The Programme of Study thus demands not only a greater and more qualitative vocabulary of movement, but also longer and more complex sequences. By implication, more links within sequences and links of greater complexity will need to be learnt. The outcome should be that confident and competent gymnasts leave the primary school, able to tackle with ease, poise and pleasure the challenges of Key Stage 3 gymnastics (11–14 years of age).

In the following sections of this chapter, some suggestions are offered to enable children to reach that potential. The first section addresses the challenge of extending the children's vocabulary of gymnastic actions, through teaching them to analyse what they can do and then build on that basic vocabulary by applying a range of *movement dimensions*, as shown in Figure 3.3 on page 61. Charts or record sheets could be used to assist the gymnasts in evaluating what they can already do. An example of a chart for analysing and developing the basic actions is shown in Figure 3.2 on page 60. The second section includes a grid (see Figure 3.4 on page 62), entitled 'Gymnastics vocabulary for building sequences and developing movement memory', which can be used in a variety of ways. It can service well the gymnast who is auditing gymnastics vocabulary, and it can be used by the teacher as a planning document or as a recording sheet for assessment. However, it was originally designed to provide an unlimited source of work for *sequence building* and the development of *movement memory*.

The ability to learn and remember sequences of gymnastics, to be able to repeat and refine them, both on the floor and using apparatus, usually challenges even the most able performer. One of the factors that can lead to early success in this is teaching children short sequences that fully meet the task set, with no superfluous movement to detract from that task. This would involve the minimum number of actions and links, such that sequences should last a maximum of up to about one minute to ensure a quality performance throughout. As gymnasts gain in strength, stamina, movement vocabulary and movement memory, longer sequences can be developed.

The chapter then continues with a focus on *apparatus*, through encouraging the auditing and extension of children's apparatus work. This section also serves as a reminder of the importance of apparatus as an essential ingredient in children's gymnastics education. For some skills, such as the forward roll, pieces of apparatus provide essential progressions towards achieving that new skill (see the section on rolling in Chapter 1). For that and other gymnastics activities, apparatus provides the obstacle to extend learning from the floor to a more difficult and challenging environment. The apparatus environment offers opportunities to work at increasingly higher levels, to work with and against gravity, to work on soft and harder surfaces, and to experience apparatus of a range of dimensions, from poles to platforms, from ladders to boxes, from ropes to benches. Actions learnt on the floor can be transferred to apparatus, and sequences built to satisfy tasks set during floorwork can be adapted and transferred to apparatus. Apparatus can often be adapted, safely, to offer a range of levels of difficulty to meet the needs of children at different stages in their learning. For example, a bar box with a platform top to the lower section can be used as one high piece or as two low pieces. A foam ramp can be rolled down in the early stages and, when experienced, can also be used to roll up. A springboard can be used both as the lowest platform on which to balance off the ground, as a means to take off in learning controlled jumping and landing and, when covered with a mat, as an incline to roll down. Apparatus also provides an additional ingredient for developing strength, flexibility, stamina and sound posture in gymnasts. Normally, apparatus work should take up at least half of the working time in each lesson, and since apparatus handling will have been mastered in Key Stage 1 (ages 5–7 years), children will need little time to set up and safety check their environment, thus allowing maximum *time on task*.

The final section of this chapter is concerned with developing partner work to a level that is at least as good as solo performance. This latter part of the chapter involves children who are working towards 'exceptional performance', who have excellent all-round personal gymnastic ability and application, and who are also very aware both of the safety requirements of working with a partner and of the need to accommodate within all work the abilities and limitations of both children.

# THE ANALYSIS AND DEVELOPMENT OF BASIC GYMNASTICS ACTIONS

Listed in Figure 3.2 on page 60 are the basic actions from the Programmes of Study for children in primary school. The chart can be used as an analysis and self-assessment task to show the level of mastery achieved in each action and the level of knowledge and understanding acquired. This chart is provided in Appendix III for you to copy and use – see Figure A.2. For each *action*, the gymnast can first *plan*, then *perform* and finally *evaluate* that action by describing or drawing the *technique* involved. The next stage would be to work on the *development* of each action by creating, performing and recording an extended movement vocabulary. The *dimensions* of body shape, direction, pathway, level, speed and rhythm, shown in Figure 3.3 on page 61, can be used to help structure those developments.

Figure 3.4 on page 62 shows the basic actions and a selection of ways of performing each action. This chart for extending movement vocabulary, developing movement memory and developing quality in gymnastics can be used in a variety of ways by both teachers and gymnasts. The teacher could use it for planning, teaching and evaluating lessons. It could also be used for recording children's completed work, or for assessment. Children could use it to plan sequences, which they could then perform and evaluate. For example, having decided on the length of the sequence, the gymnast could select the appropriate number of boxes to exemplify the theme, task or set of actions that are the focus of the lesson or unit. The boxes can then be numbered to show the plan of the sequence, as follows (see Figure 3.4 on page 62):

**1** jump, wide and extended

**2** travel on hands and feet, upside-down

**3** balance high/up

**4** roll sideways to the right.

Once practised, the gymnast could receive feedback on the work by asking another gymnast to observe the sequence and explain which boxes had been used. This activity demands both clarity and accuracy by the performer and helps to develop sound observation and explanation skills by the observer.

Alternatively, the teacher could assign sequences using the chart and, following observation of the work performed, discuss the level, suitability and accuracy of content with the gymnast.

Another approach could help gymnasts to focus on and develop their skills in linking actions. Sequences could be created by numbering boxes to indicate both the *actions* (a) of a sequence and the *links* (l) between each action. For example, the floor sequence shown again in Figure 3.4 on page 62 contains three actions and three links. Finding appropriate links from the named categories, to produce a flowing and dynamic gymnastic sequence, could be quite a challenge both for the person designing the sequence and for the performer!

| Action | Technique | Development |
|---|---|---|
| Jump and land | *Preparation: flex ankles, knees and hips, eyes looking forward, arms down and back. Action: fast extension of ankles, knees and hips. Strong push up from floor, arms swing forward and up and stop by ears, eyes looking forward, straight body. Recovery: flex ankles, knees and hips for balls of feet to land with resilience, arms swing down, eyes look forwards.* | *With wide shape then tucked shape. With leg asymmetry. With rhythm, 2 short, 1 long jump repeated. Over feet of partner's low balance.* |
| Travel on feet | | |
| Travel on hands and feet | | |
| Roll | | |
| Balance | | |
| Turn | | |
| Hang | | |
| Swing | | |
| Climb | | |

**Figure 3.2** *An analysis and self-assessment chart for basic actions in gymnastics*

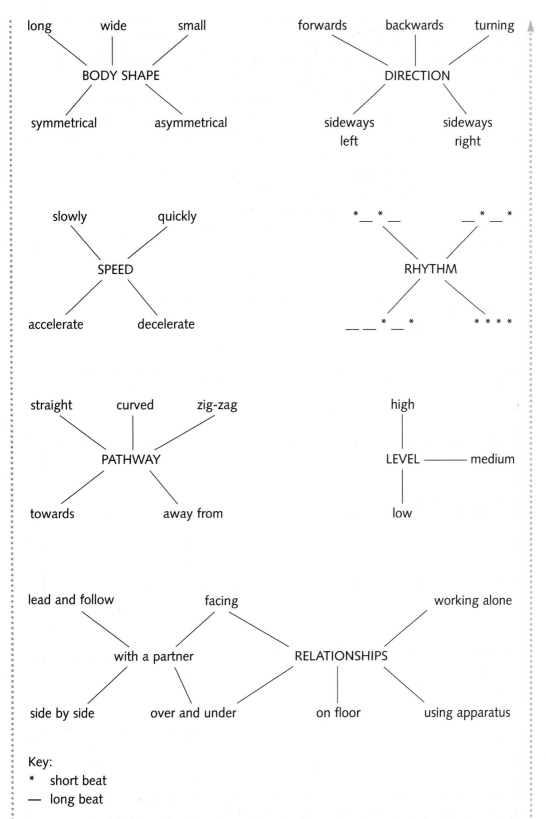

Key:
* short beat
— long beat

**Figure 3.3** *Dimensions to aid the development of basic actions*

| | Travel on feet | Travel on hands and feet | Jump and land | Roll | Balance | Turn | Pull | Push | Hang | Swing | Climb |
|---|---|---|---|---|---|---|---|---|---|---|---|
| Extended long | | | F2 | | | | | | | | |
| Extended wide | | | 1 | | | | | | | | |
| Flexed | | | | | | | | | | | |
| Symmetry | | | | | | li | | | | | |
| Asymmetry | | | | | | | | | | | |
| Forwards | | | | | | | | | | | |
| Backwards | | | | F6 | | | | | | | |
| Sideways left | a ii | | | | | | | | | | |
| Sideways right | | | | 4 | | | | | | | |
| Straight | | | | | | | a iii | | | | |
| Curved | | | | | | | | | | | |
| Zig-zag | | | | | | | | | | | |
| High/up | | | | | 3 | | | | | | A3 |
| Medium | | | | | | | | | | | |
| Low/down | | | | | | l ii | | | | | A5 |
| Slowly | | | | | | | | | | | |
| Quickly | F1 | | | | | | | | | | |
| Accelerating | | | | | | | | | | | |
| Decelerating | | | | | | | | | | | |
| Pause | | | | | l iii | | | | A4 | | |
| Rhythm | | | | | | | | | | | |
| Right way up | | | | | | | | | | | |
| Upside-down | | 2 | | | a i | | | | | | |

**Figure 3.4** *Gymnastics vocabulary for building sequences and developing movement memory*

a i    balance, upside-down

l i    turn with symmetry

a ii   travel on feet, sideways to the left

l ii   turn, low/down

a iii  pull straight

l iii  pause in balance

Encouraging gymnasts to use the floor and the apparatus for their sequences, and to focus on and select carefully the elements to be incorporated into the sequence (the travelling towards, onto and away from the apparatus elements), are further challenges to develop their experience. In the sequence shown again in Figure 3.4, F indicates an action on the floor and A indicates an action on the apparatus.

F1   travel on feet, quickly

F2   jump with extension (onto apparatus)

A3   climb up

A4   pause in hang

A5   climb down

F6   roll backwards

Were it possible to add a third dimension to this chart, the parts of the body would be added to provide the important element of *body awareness* – e.g. right foot, left foot, both feet, right hand, left hand, both hands, seat, right hip, left hip, back, front, shoulders, right side, left side, right arm, left arm, both arms. This could greatly enhance the learning opportunities and the refinement of performance by the gymnast. Such naming of the body parts responsible for leading or initiating an action or for weight-bearing during an action, would allow much closer analysis of actions and links, thereby adding further challenge and rigour to the work. (A blank copy of Figure 3.4 is reproduced in Appendix III as Figure A.3 for teachers' use.)

## Apparatus workshop – extending vocabulary

One way of extending the children's vocabulary using the apparatus is to undertake an *audit* of current practice, drawing on and recording the experience of all members of the class, in order to develop new vocabulary for each gymnast. A chart, such as that shown in Figure 3.5 on page 64, could be produced detailing the apparatus sets to be analysed (see Appendix III, Figure A.4, for a photocopiable version of this chart). A record could then be made of existing apparatus movement vocabulary, including ways of getting onto and off each piece of apparatus, as well as of ways to work on it. The audit could be done by the teacher, or by the children with the teacher.

| SET 1 Ropes | SET 2 Bar box | SET 3 Bench | SET 4 Frame |
|---|---|---|---|
| hang on one rope<br>hang upside down on two ropes<br>swing and land<br>climb up and down | | get on<br>get off<br>balance on seat, back, front<br>jump onto, off and over<br>bunny jump onto; off and over<br>roll from | |
| **SET 5 Stools Plank** | **SET 6 Cuboid and ramp** | **SET 7 Mat on springboard** | **SET 8 Tables** |
| | squat onto cuboid<br>balance on cuboid<br>roll down ramp<br>balance on ramp<br>jump from cuboid | | |

**Figure 3.5** *An audit of the apparatus vocabulary of the class*

Some of the questions to answer might be:

- Which are the easier actions to practise on this apparatus? (E.g. balancing on the matted springboard; jumping from a low table; making small shapes low down on the frame; pulling along a bench; hanging on a rope.)
- Which actions is this apparatus best suited for? (E.g. hanging, swinging, climbing on ropes; jumping onto, balancing or rolling on, and jumping from, bar box.)

Once the existing apparatus vocabulary is recorded, the next stage is to extend each child's vocabulary from that already available and observable within the class and to teach new vocabulary, to increase the total complexity and range. Some questions to answer might be:

- Which actions can some children do that others could try? (E.g. jump to land on bar box with: hands and front; hands and knees; hands and feet; hands and seat.)
- Could new actions be developed by analysing and changing the body parts used?
- Could new actions be created using changes in body shape, direction, speed, level?
- Which new sequences could be created incorporating the new actions?

**Figure 3.6** *Practising stretching*

**Figure 3.7** *Balance and hang in Key Stage 1 (ages 5–7 years)*

**Figure 3.8** *Learning small shapes in Key Stage 1 (ages 5–7 years)*

**Figure 3.9** *Fitting into holes in Key Stage 1 (ages 5–7 years)*

List below actions which extend available apparatus vocabulary:

1 _____  6 _____

2 _____  7 _____

3 _____  8 _____

4 _____  9 _____

5 _____  10 _____

# PARTNER WORK

Learning with and through the support of another person is a great way to learn and one that can be exploited to the full, particularly during childhood. From their earliest days, infants learn a great deal by copying, whether by mimicking sounds, copying speech or observing and matching a movement modelled for them. In Physical Education, teaching children to copy the movement demonstrated by the teacher is a method often used, particularly in warm-ups and when learning specific movement patterns. Learning to observe, to internalise movement and then to replicate it is a valuable tool in the movement learning process. For some children, particularly those with little body awareness, it is very difficult to match any movement modelled. Indeed, some children are unaware of the positioning of their own body and limbs unless they can actually see them. This is particularly pertinent in relation to the extremities of the body, especially the knees, ankles, wrists and fingers, the joints that are far from the brain.

The first partner in gymnastics, then, is usually the teacher, offering partnership to the whole class and providing the model that offers valuable movement observation and movement learning experience to the children. Feedback given by the teacher in this situation teaches not only movement knowledge but also vocabulary for describing and correcting movement and for establishing what is good-quality gymnastics movement. Thereafter, partner work depends on the extent and quality of the individual child's own gymnastic movement vocabulary, language development, social competence and experience in planning, performing and evaluating. Some children in Key Stage 1 are ready to work with a peer partner, but many need more time to develop their own movement vocabulary to a level that is ready for sharing, as they sometimes find that the demands of accommodating the gymnastics of another child make the experience unrewarding.

Once children are ready, a whole new learning experience opens up, to enhance not only their gymnastics but also their language and observation skills and their social development. There is no strict hierarchy of progressions in the teaching of partner work, but it is often best to start with observation and feedback, then non-contact partner work, before going on to working in contact with a partner, then in counter-balance situations and finally learning to work as a 'base' and take a partner's weight, or to work as the 'top', being supported by a partner.

The following are examples of some approaches to *partner work.*

## 1 One gymnast works, another observes and gives feedback

- The observer reports on what was seen – 'I saw John roll down the ramp'
- After observing, a simple judgement is made – 'John rolled smoothly down the ramp'
- The observer selects a point for development and gives feedback – 'John did a good sequence but he could make straighter knees in his jump'
- The observer assists a partner to improve by giving feedback during performance, as in Figures 3.10 opposite and 3.11 opposite in which Key Stage 1 children (ages 5–7 years) are helping to improve ankle extension in floorwork and Key Stage 2 children (ages 7–11 years) are working with their partners to improve the quality of performance on apparatus

**Figure 3.10** *Key Stage 1 children (ages 5–7 years) giving feedback*

**Figure 3.11** *Key Stage 2 children (ages 7–11 years) giving feedback*

## 2 Non-contact partner work

- One partner leading and the other following and copying the movement encourages careful observation and develops care in managing the space between the gymnasts, as in the photograph of sequences of travelling shown in Figure 1.1 in Chapter 1 on page 12

- Creating sequences in which the gymnasts mirror each other (see Figures 3.12 and 3.13 opposite) adds a new dimension to co-operation, to the selection of actions that each gymnast can contribute to the sequence, and to the timing of work, in sustaining synchrony

- Working towards and away from a partner provides for sequences which include both travelling and static elements and a clear floor pattern

- Using a partner as an obstacle to go over, under and around, without touching each other, challenges both gymnasts to provide appropriate high, low, and stable obstacles, and to work out safe ways of negotiating these obstacles

Once gymnasts have learnt to accommodate a partner safely and with empathy in non-contact partner work, then they should go on to learn how to work when touching or when supporting some or all of a partner's weight. Much of this work is best tackled in Key Stages 2 (ages 7–11) and 3 (ages 11–14).

## 3 Contact partner work

Holding hands, resting one hand on the partner's shoulder or touching feet together are some examples of early *contact partner work*.

- The Key Stage 1 children shown in Figure 3.14 on page 72 are balancing together on a bench with foot contact

- Where two children are of similar weight and able to co-operate successfully, they can learn to *counter-balance* by holding hands and leaning away from each other, taking care to complete the balance by leaving go of each other carefully and together. Similarly, they can use counter-balance to push up to standing together from sitting back-to-back, or to pull up to standing from sitting facing each other and holding hands. More difficult counter-balances, such as the complex counter-balance shown in Figure 3.19 on page 76, require considerable previous experience in contact partner work and in taking a partner's weight so that the base of support and the top partner are already experienced in balancing together safely.

- Supporting a partner's balance, such as with a headstand or handstand, as in Figure 3.16 on page 74, depends on the already-proven success of the gymnast's chosen balance, so that the supporter merely holds the legs to

**Figure 3.12** *Learning mirror work on the floor*

**Figure 3.13** *Learning mirror work on apparatus*

**Figure 3.14** *Contact balance on a bench*

show a controlled performance. When supporting a gymnast who is learning a headstand or handstand, the support would normally be at the hips.

- Supporting part of the partner's weight, such as in Figures 3.17 and 3.18 on page 75, initially requires good matching of partners who have knowledge, and who can give an appropriate competent performance of both the position and strength of the base and of a strong front support, and who can give an appropriate competent performance. The remaining challenges are to learn safe entries and exits and the sustaining of the front support through the arms, spine and legs. Care should always be taken to protect each other's head and to prevent collisions and falls. These gymnasts tried out a selection of entries and exits and agreed on which they would use, before attempting the whole balance. They then refined and practised the whole sequence of entry, balance and exit, before offering to perform their work. They then went on to work towards achieving this balance, fully supported as in Figure 3.20 on page 77.

- Taking the whole of a partner's weight: standing on a partner's knees, provided that the base is working on a suitably comfortable surface and the top is suitably light in weight, is probably one of the easiest balances in which the whole of a partner's weight is supported (see Figure 3.15 opposite). The balance is the right way up, relatively low down, with the centre of gravity near to the base and nearly over the base.

**Figure 3.15** *Standing on knees*

For gymnasts who have achieved the *front support balance* shown in Figures 3.17 and 3.18 on page 75, and who are ready to proceed to taking the whole of the partner's weight in a more complex balance, a sound progression would be to build up the front support with the hands on the knees of the base and the feet supported by the arms and hands of the base, as in Figure 3.20 on page 77. Again, the success of the balance depends on the knowledge, co-operation, anticipation and awareness of the two gymnasts, and on the surety of the entry, balance and exit. Figure 3.20 on page 77 shows the top partner again in front support.

**Figure 3.16** *A handstand balance*

Single balances, once learnt, should be built into sequences, with links and other actions drawn from existing movement vocabulary from solo and partner work, both on floor and using apparatus.

The leapfrog (see again Figure 1.7 in Chapter 1), where one partner makes a stable base with a high back and head tucked in and the other gymnast vaults over with hands momentarily placed on the partner's back whilst the legs straddle round the back to land, looks like an easy piece of partner work. Indeed, for many gymnasts, it is. However, it is worth rehearsing the elements integral to success, since this is a fast and quite complex action for

**Figure 3.17** *Front support, feet on shoulders*

**Figure 3.18** *Front support, legs on back*

the vaulter, involving accurate timing and position of take-off, a flight phase which uses but must not abuse the base partner, and a safe landing. Gymnasts should already be competent in the *straddle position*, the *hurdle step*

**Figure 3.19** *A counter-balance: standing on partner's knees*

and *two-footed take-off* and *straddle action,* and the *two-footed landing.* They should have gained experience of straddling over appropriate low apparatus, and should also have practised a range of positions for making a safe, stable base, before attempting this activity with a partner.

Group work in gymnastics can be introduced with great success towards the end of primary school, when gymnasts have a sound working knowledge of the basic actions and their extensions and can work with control and accuracy both alone and with a partner. Pairs or trios, performing the same sequence together on the floor or using apparatus, often make for a successful introduction to *group work,* proceeding to sequences in which the gymnasts

**Figure 3.20** *Front support on base partner's knees and hands*

follow a whole group pattern, perhaps working towards and away from a centre point. Alternatively, they might work in lines, with changes of floor pattern and direction. Working all together as well as in canon can add challenge to the sequence. Often, the use of music effectively supports the work, adding rhythm and a focus for co-ordinating the movement of each participant. Using apparatus as well as the floor adds a further challenge for the gymnasts, as does finding their own solutions, and sharing and negotiating and agreeing the content in creating sequences.

In addition to the value of group gymnastics for learning through work in progress, there is much to be learnt from opportunities for the demonstration of completed work, either as a performance to others in assembly or as a sharing exercise, perhaps with another class. Learning to retain movement in the memory, to perform to maximum potential, and to co-operate and support others, when working under the pressure of displaying, is a demanding and challenging experience that all gymnasts should experience, and in which they should also experience achievement.

## Safety in partner and group work

Learning safe practice is a general requirement within the National Curriculum for Physical Education (see the Introduction), and is particularly relevant in partner and group work, when gymnasts are required to share space in close proximity or to take part or the whole of a partner's weight. Children need to learn how to select work that is appropriate to try with the partner they have, such that both partners are safe. Partners of similar size, weight and strength are well suited to counter-balance, whereas partners of contrasting size, weight and strength may be better suited to working as base and top, where the base supports all or part of the weight of the top in each balance.

The teaching of safety in partner and group work need only be a small additional element in schools where safety education in gymnastics is established from the outset, where there is consistency of good practice and where pupils already take responsibility for themselves and show appropriate awareness of others in the variety of challenging gymnastics situations already experienced.

# Assessment, recording and reporting

In his letter to all teachers, Sir Ron Dearing writes:

'Teacher assessment is fundamental to good teaching. By making assessments during the key stage, you build up your knowledge of individual pupils' strengths and limitations, which will help you plan your teaching.'

('Physical Education – Consistency in teacher assessment, Exemplification of Standards, Key Stage 3', SCAA, 1996)

The assessment phase comes before planning (which we shall look at in the next chapter) because teachers need to know what they are going to assess before they can plan the appropriate work. Although *formal assessment* in Physical Education is a recent requirement – introduced with the National Curriculum – there has traditionally been much good practice in incorporating assessment into Physical Education planning and teaching.

Unlike most other subjects of the curriculum in which pupils' work can be collected in for marking, for correction, for feedback and for assessment, physical education learning, taking place as it does through the medium of movement, is subject to the transitory nature of that movement which is fleeting and relatively difficult to record for subsequent perusal. Teachers therefore rely on the quality of their observational skills to undertake assessment of children's learning and achievements in order to inform planning.

Good practice in assessment in gymnastics:

- is an integral part of planning, teaching, learning and evaluating
- is based upon clear learning intentions
- focuses on the learning process as well as the learning outcome

- identifies what pupils know, understand and can do
- recognises and acknowledges pupil achievements as well as weaknesses
- draws upon a wide range of evidence
- informs about individual progress
- informs future planning
- identifies realistic targets for future learning
- facilitates reporting to colleagues, parents, governors and outside agencies
- incorporates the National Curriculum Programme of Study, the Common and General Requirements and the End of Key Stage Descriptions

The *purposes* of assessing children's work include:

- to evaluate children's achievements
- to pinpoint areas for development
- to guide future planning
- to report to others
- to contribute to curriculum evaluation and review
- to contribute to curriculum planning
- to improve curriculum delivery
- to contribute to quality assurance

Those who might participate in making assessments include:

- teachers
- peers
- self: assessing one's own or others' work – or both

*Types of assessment* include:

- *continuous assessment* by the teacher, during and after lessons, to support planning and ongoing teaching
- *formative assessment* by the teacher to recognise pupil achievement and to inform future teaching and learning
- *diagnostic assessment* by the teacher to identify learning difficulties and to inform the provision of appropriately differentiated teaching
- *summative assessment* by the teacher at the end of units, schemes and phases, to report progress
- *informal* and *formal assessment* to inform the evaluation of the school's gymnastics curriculum content and delivery
- *peer assessment* by supportive class members to enhance pupil learning
- *ipsative assessment* (*self-assessment*) by the gymnasts in taking responsibility for their own progress

Methods and uses of observation include:

- observation to give immediate oral feedback
- observation to give subsequent written feedback
- use of video
- use of mirrors
- recording of own work by drawing
- recording of own work in writing
- explaining own work to another or others

As to what to assess, the End of Key Stage Descriptions describe the requirements for the end of the two phases. However, to inform those assessments and to ensure that each unit taught along the way contributes to those descriptions, the following attainments with regard to knowledge, understanding, skill and performance could be included in assessments, as appropriate, in Key Stages 1 and 2 (ages 5–7 and 7–11 years):

- the new skills learnt and the level of technical and aesthetic performance achieved
- the variety of movement vocabulary available to, and used by, the gymnast
- the accuracy and consistency of repeated performances
- the gymnast's movement memory and level of complexity of sequencing
- the gymnast's ability to plan, practise, perform and evaluate
- the gymnast's ability to observe, explain and analyse movement, and to recognise and describe quality in gymnastics
- the gymnast's understanding and application of safety
- the gymnast's floorwork, apparatus work and work on floor and apparatus together
- the gymnast's success in working with a partner and, later, in a group
- the gymnast's applications and understanding of health-related fitness
- the gymnast's ability to accept and create challenge safely and to go beyond previous experience

Towards the end of primary education and looking towards secondary education, assessment should also take account of other dimensions of gymnastic performance, including:

- body shape and line, body tension and control
- co-ordination, precision and fluency of movement
- change of direction
- change of speed
- change of level
- effectiveness of expression and use of imagination and creativity

# ▶ SELF-EVALUATION

The continuous process of Plan, Perform, Evaluate is at the centre of the spiral of learning in Physical Education. From early on in their formal schooling, most children in Key Stage 1 are well able to record their learning and to talk about what they have achieved, from their own or from a teacher-guided perspective. The Evaluation Chart (see Figure 4.1 opposite) has been successfully used with children in Years 1 and 2 (5–6 and 6–7 years of age) to record their body-awareness learning in relation to a unit of gymnastics which focused on extension and flexion of the knees and ankles. The unit was selected because these extremities of the body, being the last to develop in the cephalo-caudal (head to foot) sequence of child development, are very difficult joints for most young children to control with any certainty of accuracy, and much practice is needed to develop the knowledge and application required. Most children are successful when they can see the joints in action, but less so when relying only on sensation for feedback.

Mick, aged 6, whose work is shown in Figure 4.1, is a very able gymnast who worked hard to show to others, and to record, his gymnastic achievements and to complete the task that had been set. It is interesting to note that, although he was very accurate in the recording of his selected activities, evaluating perceptively and drawing his results in the appropriate boxes, not all of his representations actually reflect his level of performance. This is particularly so in relation to his ankles, where his 'very good' and 'good' work demonstrated sound knowledge, understanding and appropriate application of ankle extension in performance, whereas in his drawings he shows flexed ankles. He was also well able to talk about his work.

Using the Evaluation Sheet shown in Figure 4.2 on page 84, children were asked to think about all the gymnastics they had been doing recently before deciding how they wanted to answer the questions. Lili, aged 5, has ably recorded her evaluation of her gymnastics learning, achievement, pleasure and aspiration, by writing her answers. She demonstrates significant technical knowledge, understanding, discrimination and preference in her gymnastics, and observation of her during lessons show that this record is both accurate and revealing.

Such records provide valuable evidence of achievements and form a significant part of the child's ongoing gymnastics profile.

An example of a Key Stage 2 Pupil Profile of Achievement compiled during Unit 31 is shown in Figure 4.3 on page 85. Not only does this format and style offer gymnasts the opportunity to record their achievement against stated criteria, but they are also asked to give evidence from their experience and to add an action plan for future development.

**Figure 4.1** *An evaluation chart filled in by Mick, aged 6*

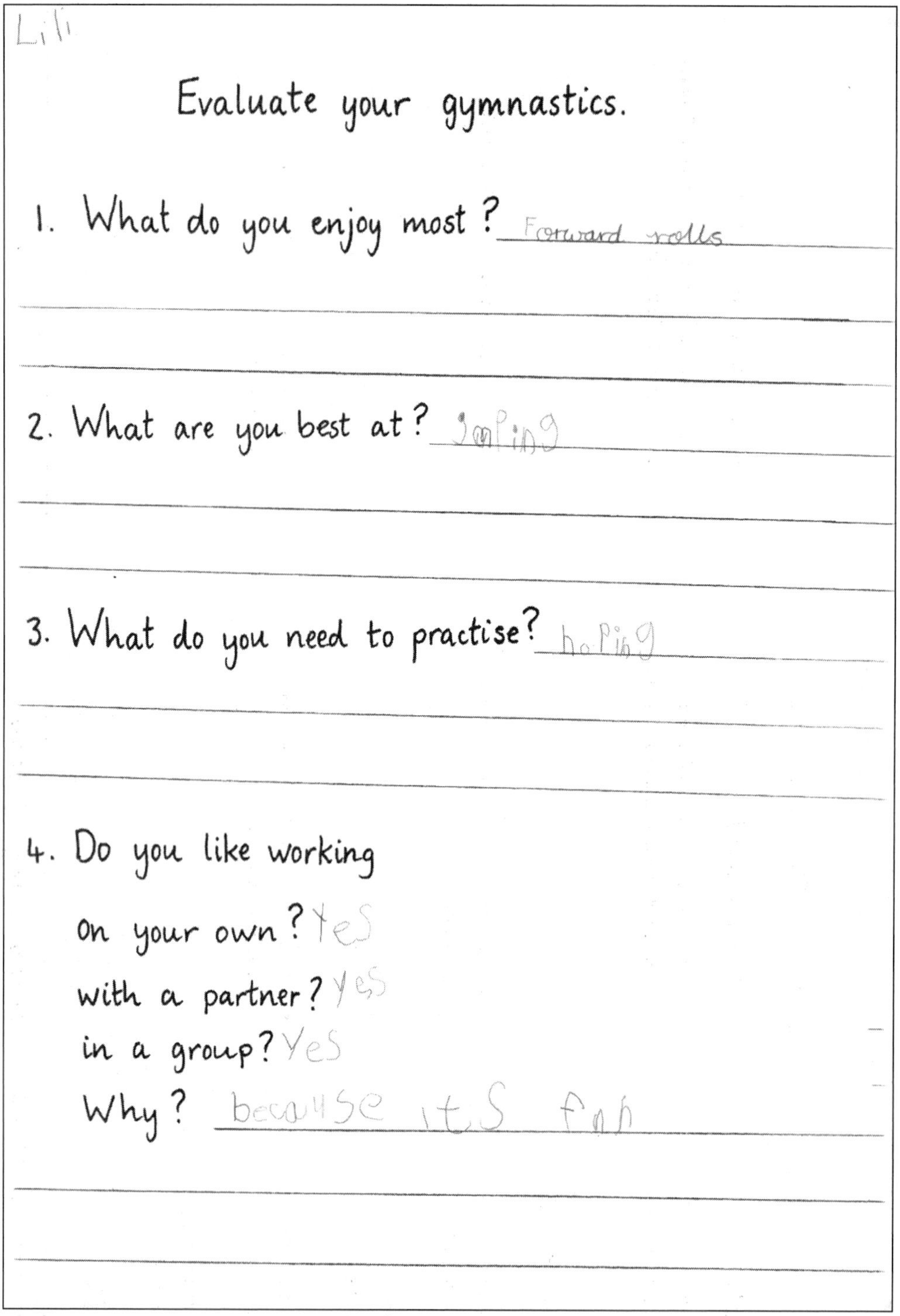

Lili

## Evaluate your gymnastics.

1. What do you enjoy most? Forward rolls

2. What are you best at? Jumping

3. What do you need to practise? hoping

4. Do you like working

   On your own? Yes
   with a partner? Yes
   in a group? Yes
   Why? because its fun

**Figure 4.2** *An evaluation chart filled in by Lili, aged 5*

## My Gymnastics Profile – Unit 31

Name _____  Class _____

| What I was taught | What I achieved | What I will try to learn next |
|---|---|---|
| to contrast speed in basic actions and links | fast jump, slow link to balance, and speed changes in one sequence | to improve my acceleration and deceleration and control in fast work |
| to contrast levels in basic actions and links | | |
| to contrast directions in basic actions and links | to incorporate work backwards in sequences | to audit directions in all my basic actions |
| to contrast body shape in basic actions and links | | |
| to increase my apparatus vocabulary | sequences with at least 3 actions on each apparatus set | I need to learn more about work upside-down |
| to work co-operatively in groups on apparatus | | |
| to use apparatus safely | | |

**Figure 4.3** *A Key Stage 2 Pupil Profile of Achievement (ages 7–11 years)*

# TEACHER ASSESSMENT

In the SCAA 1996 document, it is suggested that pupil attainment be assessed in relation to the End of Key Stage Descriptions according to the following three categories:

**1** working towards

**2** achieving

**3** working beyond.

It is also suggested that assessment be made in relation to the 'what' of achievement, where 'what' is the level of difficulty, and to the 'how' of achievement, where 'how' is the quality of that performance and its associated planning and evaluating.

In drawing up or revising your policy and practice for gymnastics assessment, a key to success is the production of an effective and manageable system, one which promotes and facilitates consistency in judgement.

The charts shown in Figures 4.4 and 4.5 on pages 88 and 89 give an example of a school's End of Key Stage 1 and End of Key Stage 2 assessments, in which the General Requirements, Programme of Study and End of Key Stage Descriptions are summarised to form a broad record of achievement of the children. The information derived from such assessments can be used both in reporting and as information to inform the planning and teaching in the next key stage. These *assessment sheets* would serve as a summary at the end of the series of units of gymnastics taught throughout the key stage, and could draw from the range of evidence accumulated as a result of pupil, peer and teacher observations and assessments undertaken during and at the end of units of work.

# CONTINUITY INTO KEY STAGE 3

The recording of achievements at the end of Key Stage 2 in order to advise the Physical Education co-ordinator in the next school can help to ensure continuity and progression into Key Stage 3 (11–14 years of age). Many secondary-school Physical Education teachers also get to know their potential students through visiting the partnership primary schools within their cluster, by working with the children and their Year 6 teacher, to experience Key Stage 2 teaching and learning, and by involving the children in Physical Education activities when they make preliminary visits to their secondary school. Sharing the school's scheme of work for Physical Education can also help the Physical Education teachers in the secondary school to understand the Key Stage 2 (ages 7–11 years) experience.

Another way of helping to ensure continuity into Key Stage 3 is for pupils to take responsibility for their own progression by keeping a *record of achievement* at Key Stage 2. This might take the form of a portfolio of experience of curricular and extra-curricular physical education or might be a summative statement of each area of the Programme of Study, or of the End of Key Stage Descriptions, mapped onto the Programme of Study. The portfolio might also include awards, badges and certificates gained, including swimming badges, athletics certificates, and photographs or videos of sport involvement.

Much can be done to value the achievements of pupils at the end of Key Stage 2, to nurture a strong self-image and to prepare them not only for the specialist facilities and Physical Education programme to be experienced at Key Stage 3, but also for what to some may be the daunting challenge of managing to remain self-motivated and to succeed in Physical Education whilst also growing physically and changing shape, body proportions and relative strength. Enabling that challenge to be met, whenever puberty is reached, is at least in part the responsibility of the Key Stage 2 teachers.

| GYMNASTICS | KEY STAGE 1 | SUMMATIVE ASSESSMENT | | | | | | |
|---|---|---|---|---|---|---|---|---|
| | **Name** | **Name** | **Name** | **Name** | **Name** | **Name** | **Name** | **Name** ...... |
| | *Tom* | | | | | | | |
| Physically active | *A* | | | | | | | |
| Positive attitude | *A* | | | | | | | |
| Safe practice | *T* | | | | | | | |
| Plan/perform/evaluate | *T* | | | | | | | |
| Travel | *B* | | | | | | | |
| Roll | *A* | | | | | | | |
| Jump | *B* | | | | | | | |
| Balance | *A* | | | | | | | |
| Swing | *A* | | | | | | | |
| Climb | *B* | | | | | | | |
| Floor | *A* | | | | | | | |
| Apparatus | *A* | | | | | | | |
| Link actions | *T* | | | | | | | |
| Repeat | *T* | | | | | | | |
| Health | *A* | | | | | | | |

Key to level of achievement: T  Working towards
                                   A  Achieving
                                   B  Working beyond

**Figure 4.4**  *An assessment chart for End of Key Stage 1*

| | GYMNASTICS | KEY STAGE 2 | SUMMATIVE ASSESSMENT | | | | |
|---|---|---|---|---|---|---|---|
| | **Name** | **Name** | **Name** | **Name** | **Name** | **Name** | **Name........** |
| | *Jane* | | | | | | |
| Physically active | *A* | | | | | | |
| Positive attitude | *A* | | | | | | |
| Safe practice | *B* | | | | | | |
| Plan/perform/evaluate | *A* | | | | | | |
| Control | *A* | | | | | | |
| Body tension | *A* | | | | | | |
| Travel | *A* | | | | | | |
| Roll | *B* | | | | | | |
| Jump | *A* | | | | | | |
| Balance | *B* | | | | | | |
| Turn | *A* | | | | | | |
| Swing | *A* | | | | | | |
| Climb | *A* | | | | | | |
| Shape | *B* | | | | | | |
| Speed | *A* | | | | | | |
| Direction | *A* | | | | | | |
| Sequence | *A* | | | | | | |
| Floor | *A* | | | | | | |
| Apparatus | *A* | | | | | | |

Key to level of achievement: T Working towards
A Achieving
B Working beyond

**Figure 4.5** *An assessment chart for End of Key Stage 2*

# Planning for gymnastics

## ► INTRODUCTION

One approach to establishing or reviewing a school's gymnastics curriculum policy, plans and practice might be to undertake an audit of existing policy, planning and practice and then to set new developments both within the context of current best practice and within the whole curriculum policy of the school.

One method of auditing would be to take account of the school's existing involvement in gymnastics by examining the following aspects of current practice:

- the curriculum aims and policy for gymnastics
- the scheme of work for gymnastics throughout the school
- the gymnastics assessment scheme
- teaching styles and teaching strategies for effective learning
- skills, abilities, strengths and areas for development of the teachers
- continuing professional development provision for the teachers
- pupils' movement development, including the techniques of gymnastics
- pupils' language development, including the technical language of gymnastics
- levels of gymnastics achievement of the pupils, in terms of skills, knowledge and understanding
- the availability of the hall or other teaching space
- the overall allocation of sessions to gymnastics each year, by term, by week and by day
- the number and distribution of sessions per term for each class/age group
- the length of each teaching session for each class/age group

- the provision of apparatus both fixed and portable
- apparatus storage, access and availability
- whole-school practices in relation to safety, dress and footwear, apparatus management
- the use of IT, including video feedback
- resources, including books, charts and videos for teachers and for pupils
- networking with other schools to maximise expertise
- extra-curricular provision within the school and within the community

# RECEPTION AND KEY STAGE 1

## Overall aims for gymnastics

- to introduce pupils to the environment, movement vocabulary, resources and language of gymnastics
- to provide for the achievement of mature movement patterns in locomotion, jumping, balance and agility, and to facilitate effective body management and co-ordination
- to teach the National Curriculum Programme of Study, with relevant elements of the Common and General Requirements
- to enable pupils to achieve the End of Key Stage Descriptions by the end of Year 2 (6–7 years of age)
- to provide a developmental, challenging, progressive and attainable gymnastics learning experience for each pupil
- to establish school policy with regard to practices and routines for apparatus handling and for safety in gymnastics

## Long-term planning

This is whole-school, Key Stage or phase planning in which the broad framework is drawn up to indicate the school's overall aims and objectives for the achievement of the National Curriculum for Gymnastics. Decisions are made about the distribution of gymnastics teaching through the school and about the allocation of units of work to classes, through the three terms of the year – see Table 5.1 on page 92. These, along with the broad content of units, potential time provision and the assessment focus for each unit, constitute the essentials of long-term plans.

To cater for the particular needs of young children in terms of motor development, body management and co-ordination, the allocation of units

| Year | Autumn Term | Spring Term | Summer Term |
|------|-------------|-------------|-------------|
| Reception | Unit 1 | Unit 3 | Unit 5 |
| Reception | Unit 2 | Unit 4 | Unit 6 |
| 1 | Unit 7 | Unit 8 | Unit 9 |
| 1 | Unit 10 | Unit 11 | Unit 12 |
| 2 | Unit 13 | Unit 14 | Unit 15 |
| 2 | Unit 16 | Unit 17 | Unit 18 |

**Table 5.1** *Allocation of units for Reception and Key Stage 1*

should ideally be on a continuous rather than on a blocked basis, so that regular and frequent teaching can allow for the gradual acquisition, practice and consolidation of skills, knowledge and understanding. Therefore, the plan shown in Table 5.2, which provides for two units per term in each of the three terms of the three years, allows adequate time for the majority of pupils to complete the Programme of Study and achieve the End of Key Stage Descriptions.

If each of the 18 units shown in Table 5.1 is made up of six sessions, if one session is taught each week and each session is between 20 and 30 minutes of activity time, according to the needs of the class, then continuity would be achieved and the Programme of Study for Key Stage 1 could be covered in addition to addressing the End of Key Stage Descriptions as well as relevant aspects of the Common and General Requirements, as shown in Table 5.2 on pages00 93 and 94.

## Medium-term planning

The recommendations given in SCAA 1995 (see the Bibliography at the end of the book) indicate that the learning objectives for units of work should be set out, along with teaching strategies, provision for differentiation and assessment opportunities. From the Long-Term Plans for Gymnastics in Reception and Key Stage 1 outlined in Tables 5.1 and 5.2, the Medium-Term Plan for the first unit of work in the Autumn term for Year 1 (ages 5–6 years) is now outlined in Table 5.3 on page 95. This unit is designed to be taught in six lessons, and culminates in a sharing of work.

| Year | Unit | Programme of Study: Content | Common and General Requirements | End of Key Stage Descriptions |
|------|------|-----------------------------|--------------------------------|-------------------------------|
| Reception | 1 | Introduction to the hall space<br>Travel on feet, and on hands and feet<br>Apparatus management<br>Learn how to get on and off apparatus | 1a: physically active | Perform simple skills safely |
| Reception | 2 | Body awareness, whole body travel, jump, roll, balance<br>Apparatus management<br>Ways of getting on and off apparatus | 3a: respond to instructions,<br>1a | Perform simple skills safely |
| Reception | 3 | Body awareness, legs, hips, knees and ankles, floor and apparatus | 1a, 3a,<br>2d: mindful of others | Work alone<br>Talk about own work |
| Reception | 4 | Body awareness, arms, shoulders, elbows and wrists, floor and apparatus | 1a, 3a, 2d,<br>3d: lift, carry, place and use equipment safely | Perform simple skills safely |
| Reception | 5 | Body shape, control in shape-making, floor and apparatus | 1a, 2d, 3a, 3d | Plan and perform simple skills safely |
| Reception | 6 | Body shape, control in shape-making while moving<br>Linking actions, on floor and apparatus | 1a, 2d, 3a, 3d | Work alone<br>Talk about own work |
| 1 | 7 | Travel on hands and feet<br>Examine body shapes<br>Ankle extension<br>Linking actions on floor<br>Ways of getting on and off apparatus | 1a, 2d, 3a, 3d,<br>2c: consolidate performance | As for Reception Units 1–6 above<br>Talk about own work<br>Observe partner |
| 1 | 8 | Rolling, travelling and body shapes as balances, floor and apparatus | 1a, 2c, 2d, 3a ,3d | Talk about own work |

**Table 5.2** *Unit planning for Reception and Key Stage 1 (Continues overleaf)*

| Year | Unit | Programme of Study: Content | Common and General Requirements | End of Key Stage Descriptions |
|---|---|---|---|---|
| 1 | 9 | Jump and land, Rolling and travelling Linking above actions floor and apparatus | 1b: posture and use of body | Judge own work Observe partner |
| 1 | 10 | Balancing Jump, land and roll Links floor and apparatus | 1a, 2c, 2d, 3a, 3d | Talk about and judge own work |
| 1 | 11 | Revision of jump, land, balance, hang, swing and climb Linking of basic actions Floor and apparatus | 1a, 1b, 2c, 2d, 3a, 3d | Plan and perform simple skills safely Talk about and judge own work |
| 1 | 12 | Develop linking of jump, land, balance, travel, hang, swing, climb Observe a partner Floor and apparatus | 1a, 2c plan, perform, evaluate | Linking Talk about and judge partner's work |
| 2 | 13 | Develop jump, land, roll and balance Floor and apparatus | 1c: cardio-vascular health, flexibility, muscular strength, endurance | Effects of exercise Partner feedback |
| 2 | 14 | Linking of actions Sequence building Floor and apparatus | 1a, 1b, 2c, 2d, 3d, 3e: warm up for and recovery from exercise | Control in linking |
| 2 | 15 | Develop vocabulary of linking movements, Work with a partner Movement memory Floor and apparatus | 1b, 1c, 2c, 2d, 3a, 3d, 3e, 1d: personal hygiene | All aspects of EKSD |
| 2 | 16 | Quality of movement Performance of sequences Floor and apparatus | Consolidate all elements above | All aspects of EKSD |

| | Learning objectives | Teaching strategies | Differentiation | Assessment focus |
|---|---|---|---|---|
| 1 | Examine travel on feet<br>Revise shapes with stretched ankles<br>Link actions on floor<br>Learn ways of getting onto and off apparatus | Class teaching of jog, hop, skip, gallop<br>Independent work on shapes with stretched ankles | Range of resilience of travel<br>Variety and complexity of shapes with ankle extension<br>Range of independence | Quality of control of travel and ankle extension<br>Safe practice<br>Independent work |
| 2 | Examine shapes on hands and feet<br>Revise travel on feet<br>Link actions<br>Floor and apparatus | Class teaching of hands and feet shapes, back up, tummy up, turning over<br>Independent work on feet | Range of shapes on hands and feet<br>Variety and complexity of travel on feet | Quality of control of travel on hands and feet<br>Safe practice |
| 3 | Revise body shapes – stretched, straight, tucked<br>Link travel and shape<br>Floor and apparatus | Independent work with pupil demonstrations<br>Class teach<br>Revise apparatus management | Variety of movement vocabulary and body shapes<br>Range of tension in shapes<br>Ability to manage apparatus co-operation | Consolidation of performance<br>Vocabulary and body tension<br>Skill in lifting, carrying, placing and using apparatus |
| 4 | Develop travel on feet<br>Develop travel, link, shape<br>Floor and apparatus | Class teaching of walk, run, trot, gallop<br>Independent work | Quality of performance<br>Variety of movement vocabulary | Quality of performance and safe practice<br>Movement vocabulary<br>Apparatus management |
| 5 | Develop travel on hands and feet<br>Choose and practise 1 each of straight, star, tuck shapes<br>Floor and apparatus<br>Link actions | Class teaching of bunny jump to travel and start low cartwheel action<br>Independent work<br>Use of apparatus to develop bunny jump and cartwheel actions | Development of alternate actions of feet and hands<br>Range of apparatus available | Development of alternate action on floor and on apparatus<br>Talk about own work<br>Safe practice |
| 6 | Sharing of best travel on feet, hands and feet, and of best straight, star, tuck shapes<br>Share linked work<br>Floor and apparatus | Partner observation<br>Observation and feedback on individual performance | Range and complexity of vocabulary selected | Consolidation of performance |

**Table 5.3** *Medium-term plan for Key Stage 1, Year 1, Autumn Term, Unit 7*

# Short-term planning

The SCAA (1995) recommendation is that weekly or daily plans and records should ensure effective teaching and assessment. These plans should include suitably differentiated activities based on clear objectives.

The lesson plan shown in Table 5.4 on pages 98 and 99 is based on the following information:

- learning objectives
- criteria for the assessment of pupils' learning
- organisational details
- a four-section framework to the lesson structure
- tasks for pupils in each section
- observation and feedback notes for the teacher to improve the quality of the pupils' performance
- details of management and safety
- an apparatus plan

The lesson is structured in four interrelated parts :

1 *warm up*. This comprises the introductory activities that prepare pupils for the session and address the following objectives:
   - cardio-vascular preparation
   - preparation of the joints (hips, knees, ankles, shoulders, elbows, wrists, fingers, the spine and all the muscles serving those joints)
   - weight-bearing activities on the feet, hands and feet, and other parts of body
   - non-weight-bearing activities, swinging, circling, flexing, extending joints
   - work on the spot and through the space
   - use of the whole room space, establishment of spatial awareness
   - establishing personal behaviour management and safe practice
   - establishing concentration and focus on the objectives of the session

2 *floorwork*. The content of the session here comprises tasks which develop the objectives of the lesson and increase the movement vocabulary, complexity and quality of the pupils' gymnastics. These tasks include *single actions*, *links* and *sequences*, and lead to the apparatus work. They are also structured to satisfy the assessment criteria.

3 *apparatus work*. In addition to the demands of learning to *lift, carry, place, set up* and *dismantle* and *replace* apparatus, pupils here learn to co-operate with others, to check the safety of the apparatus and to use it to improve their

gymnastics. They should be taught many ways of getting onto and off apparatus. This apparatus work should develop out of the preceding floorwork, should extend it and should add challenge.

Apparatus sets should be designed in advance of the session so that apparatus can be arranged in accessible locations around the sides of the hall. The arrangement should be appropriate both for the age and ability of the children and for the tasks in hand. When experienced, children should learn to design their own apparatus sets.

**4**  *conclusion.* Once the apparatus has been replaced, pupils should review the session against the learning objectives, share new learning, check posture, cool down, set future targets and prepare to return to the changing rooms or classroom.

### Short-term plan for Key Stage 1, Year 1, Unit 7, Lesson 1

Throughout this lesson, the major focus will be on safe, challenging physical activity, with maximum time spent on the task and minimum time spent on waiting, non-gymnastic activity or teacher management of space, behaviour or apparatus.

The organisational details are as follows:

- *32 children:*
  - changing, lesson objectives, and assessment criteria, apparatus-handling groups and preparation for warm-up completed in the classroom
  - walk to hall, leave shoes in storage area at door, enter and start work.

- *objectives:*
  - to teach travel actions on feet;
  - to improve the awareness and quality of ankle extension in shape-making;
  - to lift, carry, place and use apparatus safely.

- *criteria for assessment:*
  - vocabulary of travel shown;
  - ability to extend ankles in shapes when watching and when not able to see ankles
  - ability to lift, carry, place and use apparatus safely.

- *grouping:*
  - working alone. New groups for apparatus handling.

- *apparatus:*
  - individual mats in four corners;
  - apparatus sets stored at the sides of the hall, for easy access. See Apparatus Plan on page 109.

| Pupil tasks | Teacher feedback to develop quality | Management and safety |
| --- | --- | --- |
| *Warm up* | | |
| On the spot, jogging | Resilient, listen to feet, upright posture | Large personal space Work on the spot 'Rest' is stopping word |
| Circle one arm, other arm, both arms, backwards and forwards | Steady, straight posture Keep body still, just use arms | In large personal space Facing me, copy |
| Jogging on the spot | Quick, quiet feet, get out of breath | |
| *Floorwork* | | |
| Bounce to new places | On 2 feet, small, neat jumps Straight posture, tidy arms | Look for a clear space Keep away from others |
| Hop, gallop, skip to new places | Tidy feet, legs, posture | Eyes looking for clear spaces |
| Practise hopping | Jump high on one foot, other leg tidy, arms tidy, straight posture | Eyes looking forward Go where no-one else goes |
| Collect mat from nearest corner, sit beside it | Place mat softly in big space Tidy posture | Take care at mat stack Take turns to collect mat |
| Sit on mat, with straight legs Tidy posture | Extend ankles, knees flat on floor Push toes away from you | Sit softly, in own space Look at knees and ankles |
| Make new shapes with stretchy ankles | On back or tummy or on hands and feet | Stay in own space |
| Choose and practise best shape | Are your ankles extended, body stretched? | Hold shape, stop, repeat |
| Travel round mat by hopping, make best shape on mat. Repeat | Tidy, soft travel Smooth shape-making Show clear shape | Stay near own mat and away from others as you travel |
| Sit beside nearest person Watch partner | Quickly, quietly Look for good hops and stretched ankles in shape | Check twos Spacing and safety for observation |
| Who did/saw good hops, stretched ankles? | Sitting, hands up | Observe sequencing |
| Change over, new worker, new watcher | Repeat tasks for worker and observer | Check on task and safety |

**Table 5.4** *Short-term plan for Key Stage 1, Year 1, Unit 7, Lesson 1*

| Pupil tasks | Teacher feedback to develop quality | Management and safety |
|---|---|---|
| Who did/saw good hops, stretched ankles? | Remind children of quality of hop, shape of stretched ankles | Put mat away on same stack and sit by partner |

*Apparatus*

| | | |
|---|---|---|
| Set up apparatus Sit down in space Look for safety | Check lifting, location of each set Away from apparatus Teacher check safety | Classroom assistant help  Assistant check safety |
| Practise ways of getting onto and off apparatus | Move from set to set to show getting on and off | Avoid queues, encourage wide vocabulary |
| Get on apparatus, show stretched ankles, get off | Choose clear place on apparatus Both ankles extended | Check safe spacing Check on task |
| Bounce to new apparatus, get on, show stretched ankles, get off | Soft bouncing, look for a place Get on carefully, stretch both ankles | Safety during travel Avoid crowding on apparatus |
| Sit down, look at ankles | Ankles extended, good posture | Sitting on floor (not on mats or apparatus) |
| Now try bouncing and shape-making with stretched ankles | Travel softly, show clear shape | Safety during travel, space for shape, careful getting on and off |
| Sit in apparatus groups Put apparatus away | Beside apparatus you put out Same order. Care in group | Check groups Check lifting, moving, putting down apparatus Classroom assistant helps |

*Conclusion*

| | | |
|---|---|---|
| Sit with stretchy ankles | Good posture | In a space |
| Stand up with tidy posture | Straight body, eyes looking forward, tall shape, hands by sides, and feet together | |
| What have you learnt? | Review criteria for assessment | |
| Blue T-shirts, walk to shoes, then red T-shirts etc Stand in class line Walk to changing area | Send by T-shirt colour or other distinguishing feature Space between you and next person | Check no crowding Quiet return to changing area |

**Table 5.4** *Short-term plan for Key Stage 1, Year 1, Unit 7, Lesson 1*

# KEY STAGE 2

## Overall aims for gymnastics

- to build upon the pupils' existing gymnastics abilities, skills, knowledge and understanding
- to teach the National Curriculum Programme of Study for Gymnastics, with relevant elements of the Common and General Requirements
- to enable pupils to achieve the End of Key Stage Descriptions by the end of Year 6 (10–11 years of age)
- to develop pupils' skills of observation and critical analysis in planning, performing and evaluating, and to encourage independence and peer co-operation in learning
- to provide an attainable, active, challenging and satisfying learning experience for pupils
- to instil safe practice
- to enable pupils to move to Key Stage 3 (11–14 years of age) as confident and competent gymnasts

## Long term planning

At Key Stage 2 (ages 7–11 years), in order to provide for the six areas of Physical Education to be taught, it may not be possible to include two units of gymnastics in each term throughout the year. Whilst continuity in gymnastics learning is preferable, it may therefore be necessary to move to blocks of units as shown in Table 5.5 opposite, where the Autumn and Spring Term work is continuous and where, in the Summer Term, other areas of the Programmes of Study, such as Athletics and Outdoor and Adventurous Activities make up the Physical Education curriculum.

The allocation of units shown in Table 5.5 should ensure that children receive a worthwhile gymnastics learning opportunity and the opportunity to achieve the levels of competence that will enable them to proceed with confidence to Key Stage 3.

If each of the 16 units shown in Table 5.5 is made up of six sessions, if one session is taught each week and each session comprises 30 minutes of activity time, then sufficient continuity could be achieved and the Programme of Study for Key Stage 2 could be covered in addition to addressing the End of Key Stage Descriptions as well as relevant aspects of the Common and General Requirements, as shown in Table 5.6 opposite.

| Year | Autumn Term | Spring Term | Summer Term |
|------|-------------|-------------|-------------|
| 3 | Unit 19 | Unit 21 | |
| 3 | Unit 20 | Unit 22 | |
| 4 | Unit 23 | Unit 25 | |
| 4 | Unit 24 | Unit 26 | |
| 5 | Unit 27 | Unit 29 | |
| 5 | Unit 28 | Unit 30 | |
| 6 | Unit 31 | Unit 33 | |
| 6 | Unit 32 | Unit 34 | |

**Table 5.5** *Allocation of units for Key Stage 2 (ages 7–11 years)*

| Year | Unit | Programme of Study: Content | Common and General Requirements | End of Key Stage Descriptions |
|------|------|-----------------------------|---------------------------------|-------------------------------|
| 3 | 19 | Warm up, sustain energetic activity Jump land, roll, changes in body shape Start sequencing Floor and apparatus | 1a: physical activity 1b: posture and use of body 3a: respond to instructions | Sustain energetic activity Plan and perform simple skills safely |
| 3 | 20 | Revise warm-up knowledge Sequence jump, land, roll, with change of direction and shape Examine turn Floor and apparatus Swing and climb on apparatus | 1c: cardio-vascular health, flexibility, muscular strength, endurance 1a, 1b, 3a, plan, perform, evaluate | Effects of exercise Practise, improve, refine performance Increase control |
| 3 | 21 | Travel on hands and feet, with change of speed, shape, direction Balance, turn Sequencing Floor and apparatus | 2c: consolidate performance 3d: lift, carry, place and use apparatus safely 3b: safety procedures | Judge own performance, to improve |
| 3 | 22 | Revise balance and turn Start partner work Sequencing Floor and apparatus Start profile of gymnastics achievements and targets Share completed sequences | Language development 2d: mindful of others 2a: sporting behaviour 3d | Judge other's performance |

**Table 5.6** *Unit planning for Key Stage 2 (ages 7–11 years) (continued overleaf)*

| Year | Unit | Programme of Study: Content | Common and General Requirements | End of Key Stage Descriptions |
|---|---|---|---|---|
| 4 | 23 | Develop warm up Develop weight on hands with travel and balance Floor and apparatus sequences | 3e: warm up and recovery from exercise 3c: safety risks 3a, 3b | Find solutions to challenges Increase control |
| 4 | 24 | Audit basic actions Floor and apparatus Develop partner work Floor and apparatus Practise and improve sequences | 2b: cope with success and limitations 2a, 2c, 2d, plan, perform, evaluate | Judge own and others' performance Refine performance |
| 4 | 25 | Increase complexity of sequences of basic actions, changes of shape, speed, direction, level | 1a, 1b, 1c, 1d | Work safely alone Improve accuracy, quality and variety of performance |
| 4 | 26 | Prepare partner sequence with more complex actions and links on floor and apparatus Performance of sequences Record achievements and set targets | 2b, 2c, 2d, 3d | Increase quality Work safely in pairs Judge performance |
| 5 | 27 | Audit movement vocabulary of basic actions, extend vocabulary Research potential of apparatus Design apparatus sets for tasks | 3e, 3a, 3b, 3c, 3d, plan, perform, evaluate | Find solutions to challenges Work safely Sustain energetic activity |
| 5 | 28 | Audit movement vocabulary of links. New links into and out of basic actions on floor and apparatus Work on new vocabulary of actions | 1a, 1b, 1c, 1d | Respond imaginatively, find solutions |

**Table 5.6** *Unit planning for Key Stage 2 (ages 7–11 years) (continued)*

| Year | Unit | Programme of Study: Content | Common and General Requirements | End of Key Stage Descriptions |
|---|---|---|---|---|
| 5 | 29 | Examine types of partner work using complex actions and links | Plan, perform, evaluate | Find solutions to challenges |
| | | Create sequences on floor and apparatus | 2a, 2b, 2c, 2d | Improve accuracy of performance Judge other's |
| 5 | 30 | Audit and record own achievements in relation to the Programme of Study | Plan, perform, evaluate | Refine performance Judge own work |
| | | Set personal targets for Year 6 on floor and apparatus | 2b, 2c, 2d | Sustain energetic activity |
| 6 | 31 | Develop contrasts in basic actions and links to increase complexity of sequences Research potential of apparatus, and add new vocabulary | 3a, 3b, 3c, 3d, 3e | Improve accuracy, quality and variety of performance |
| 6 | 32 | Prepare and perform partner sequences incorporating complex actions and links floor and apparatus Start gymnastics profile | 2a, 2b, 2c, 2d | Find solutions to challenges Increase control |
| 6 | 33 | Develop and perform complex sequences, working alone on floor and apparatus Continue gymnastics profile | All aspects of the Common and General requirements | All aspects of the EKSD |
| 6 | 34 | Develop and perform complex sequences working in groups Floor and apparatus Complete gymnastics profile | Plan, perform, evaluate | Judge other's performance |

**Table 5.6** *Unit planning for Key Stage 2 (ages 7–11 years) (continued)*

| | Learning objectives | Teaching strategies | Differentiation | Assessment |
|---|---|---|---|---|
| 1 | Examine basic actions for own level of complexity<br>Audit work on floor and apparatus | Class teaching of actions<br>Individual profile of complexity<br>Individual work on apparatus | Selection of vocabulary<br>Style of recording<br>Range of apparatus vocabulary | Quality of actions selected<br>Level of potential achieved<br>Ability to consolidate performance at level of potential |
| 2 | Examine linking movements, including twist<br>Audit range of links<br>Develop sequence of best links between actions<br>Floor and apparatus | Class teaching of links into and out of selected basic actions<br>Individual practice to audit<br>Individual creation of sequences | Control in links | Quality of sequencing<br>Appropriateness of links<br>Quality of selected links |
| 3 | Progression in partner work: lead and follow, mirror<br>Create sequences of lead and follow and mirror<br>Floor and apparatus | Class teaching of lead and follow and mirror<br>Pairs plan, perform, evaluate | Level of awareness of partner in spacing and vocabulary | Quality of partner co-operation<br>Ability to maintain own quality |
| 4 | Revise lead and follow<br>Introduce partner as obstacle in non-contact work<br>Floor and apparatus | Pairs practise lead and follow<br>Class teach over and under<br>Evaluate partner and sequences | Range of gymnastics<br>Variety of vocabulary used<br>Accuracy of performance | Quality of range of content<br>Care of partner, awareness |
| 5 | Introduce contact partner work, touching balances, balance with counter-tension<br>Sequences, including selected balances<br>Floor and apparatus | Class teaching of contact balances<br>Pairs development of vocabulary of balances and links | Introduce simple and complex attainable balances<br>Range of entries to and exits from balances | Ability to accept challenge and to consolidate work<br>Quality of balances, links and peer feedback |
| 6 | Create sequences for performance<br>Observe and judge others | Pairs select type of partner work<br>Assessment and oral feedback | Free choice of sequence content<br>Level of analysis | Summative assessment of performance and peer support<br>Quality of assessment of others |

**Table 5.7** *Medium-term plan for Key Stage 2, Year 5, Spring Term, Unit 29*

# Medium-term planning

Medium-Term Planning should include the objectives for each unit of work, the assessment criteria, teaching strategies and provision for differentiation.

Whilst a unit might follow the structure and even the content of the following example, the importance of designing units to meet the needs of teachers and pupils in the school cannot be over-estimated.

Table 5.7 opposite shows a development of Unit 29, Year 5, Spring Term.

# Short-term planning

For details of lesson structure, refer again to pages 96 and 97. The following is an example of a single session, taught within a unit as described in Tables 5.6 and 5.7. As with Medium-Term Planning, it is preferable for teachers to write their own plans in order to meet the needs of their pupils and the particular circumstances of their school.

### Short-term plan for Key Stage 2, Year 5, Unit 29, Lesson 4

The organisational details are as follows:

- *34 children*:
  - dress, pairs, objectives, warm-up preparation completed before entry to hall; non-participant pupil with observation sheet and pencil to record partner work.

- *apparatus*:
  - arranged around edges of hall for easy access, mats on trolley – use Figure 5.2.

- *objectives*:
  - to extend partner work, lead and follow, mirror, partner as obstacle;
  - to increase vocabulary of basic actions and links through partner co-operation;
  - to increase experience of peer tutoring and peer feedback.

- *criteria for assessment*:
  - ability to create and perform sequences on floor and apparatus, working with partner as obstacle;
  - quality of peer tutoring and feedback.

| Pupil tasks | Teacher feedback to develop quality | Management and safety |
|---|---|---|
| *Warm up* | | |
| Jogging, follow partner | Resilient feet, tidy posture | Look, avoid others |
| Travel, other partner leading | Copy exactly, get out of breath | Leave space between self and partner |
| Change leader, travel | Select activity partner can do | |
| Circle arms, stretch at shoulders | Straight posture, arms by ears | Facing partner |
| | Hold stretch, check partner | Check spacing |
| Stretch at waist and hips | Hold stretch, try to be exact | Check partner work |
| *Floorwork* | | |
| Leave partner and work alone | | |
| Make, strong high bridges that a partner could go under | On hands and feet, back up, front up, side up, | Check personal space |
| | Hold shape | |
| Practise actions for going under | Pull, push, roll | |
| One partner make bridges, other partner go under | Hold bridge until partner is through | Avoid touching partner |
| Change over | Go under the tallest bridge | Evaluate partner |
| Make low strong shapes that partner could go over | Front support, back support, side support | Plan for partner to go over the 'foot end' |
| Practise actions for going over low shapes | Step, jump, bunny jump roll, cartwheel | Gauge height needed to clear partner's shape |
| One partner make shapes other partner go over | Hold shape until partner is over | Safe spacing, no contact |
| | Show resilience in landings | Go over 'foot end' of partner |
| Change over | Show clarity of shape with body tension | |
| Alternatively make bridges and go over or under partner's bridges | Build a repeatable sequence of shapes and actions to go over or under partner. Transfer smoothly | Check safety Monitor and assess quality of sequence |
| Select best content for sequence, practise | Suggest 2 bridges, 1 'over' and 1 'under' each. Teach links and continuity. Encourage accuracy, control and efficiency No superfluous movement | Encourage pathways to avoid others Evaluate each other's work |
| *Apparatus* | | |
| Set up apparatus as before | Appropriate handling, suitable spacing. Check safety of sets | Check lifting, carrying, co-operating, spacing |
| Visual safety check | | |

**Table 5.8** *Short-term plan for Key Stage 2, Year 5, Unit 29, Lesson 4 (continued opposite)*

| Pupil tasks | Teacher feedback to develop quality | Management and safety |
|---|---|---|
| Alone, find places to make balances for partner to go over safely | On apparatus, or floor and apparatus<br>Hold balance strongly | Spacing of sets and safe working |
| One partner make balance, other partner go over without touching | Keep foot end of balance low<br>Go over from floor or from apparatus | Ensure safe balances, non-contact actions and landings |
| Use floor and apparatus to create a sequence of alternate balance and action to go over partner's balance | Encourage peer tutoring and peer feedback, one gymnast teaching another and one pair teaching another<br>Encourage economy of movement | Ensure appropriate activity level and on-task activity |
| Show sequence and report | Feedback on content and quality | Observers in suitable space |
| Apparatus away | Praise efficient, careful work | Check safety |
| *Conclusion*<br>Check partner's posture in sitting and standing | Encourage straight shape, relaxed, symmetry in legs and arms | Check peer tutoring |
| Review learning against assessment criteria | | |
| Prepare to leave hall | Summary of achievements | Check hall |

**Table 5.8** *Short-term plan for Key Stage 2, Year 5, Unit 29, Lesson 4*

# MAXIMISING APPARATUS

To make the most of the limited time available for developing work on apparatus, and to enable children to maximise the potential of each piece of apparatus, curriculum planners should consider the following points:

- Store the apparatus round the edges of the hall during the working day, so that it is readily accessible for the children
- Involve additional adults in assisting young children as they learn to handle apparatus
- Design apparatus sets that enable the maximum, simultaneous, safe use of each piece

- Plan to involve the maximum number of safely spaced sets in every lesson
- Encourage children to work across long apparatus (such as ladders, benches), thereby providing several children with a work space on each piece at the same time, and minimising the need for queueing or waiting for turns
- Design apparatus sets that best suit the children's experience, height and strength, and which best serve the objectives of the unit
- Allocate children to the same apparatus-handling groups for entire units or until they are familiar with the management of that apparatus
- Teach children to co-operate to lift, carry and set up their own apparatus, from their first days in school
- Minimise the time spent on teacher administration of apparatus, by adopting and practising a whole-school policy for the routines of efficiency and safety in apparatus handling and management, by using task cards for older pupils and by maintaining consistently high levels of expectation of pupils in relation to safe practice, co-operation and behaviour management
- Teach the children to:
  - move freely around all the apparatus sets, wherever there is a suitable space, approaching, using and leaving that apparatus from a variety of positions;
  - work in groups which remain at the same apparatus set, to develop or to complete a piece of work;
  - use all the apparatus available;
  - use mats to designate landing areas, for assisting resilience when landing from a height, or for denoting areas to practise working upside-down, including rolling.

## Apparatus provision

For the Key Stage 1 and Key Stage 2 lessons (ages 5–7 and 7–11 respectively) (see Tables 5.4 and 5.8) described on pages 98 and 106, the following *apparatus plans* were used:

## Apparatus plan for Key Stage 1, Unit 7

For this unit, in which travel and shape-making are the focus, it is important to provide:

- maximum floor area around each piece of apparatus, to allow for many routes to be available for approaching and leaving each set in the travel component;

- as much low apparatus as possible to enable children to get on and off each piece easily, so that most attention could be given to practising shapes on the apparatus;

- the maximum number of individual low surfaces for shape-making so that every child can concentrate on the quality of body shape as they work;

- the maximum range of apparatus overall, including fixed apparatus such as ropes and frames, to encourage shape-making not only on flat, stable surfaces but also on the less stable surface of foam equipment, on slopes, on vertical apparatus and under apparatus, such as high movement tables, as appropriate.

See Figure 5.1.

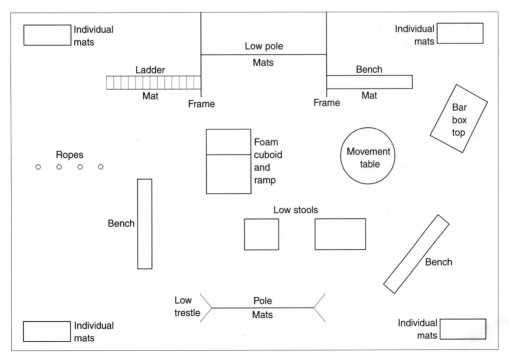

**Figure 5.1** *Apparatus plan for Key Stage 1, Unit 7*

## Apparatus plan for Key Stage 2, Unit 29

For this unit, in which the focus is on non-contact partner work, creating obstacles and going over those obstacles, it is important to provide:

- sufficient apparatus for each pair of children to have sufficient space to practise obstacle making and to find a variety of ways to go over those obstacles
- apparatus that offers the potential for the feet to be low, so that gymnasts can negotiatethe apparatus and each other safely
- apparatus and mats that facilitate landing after going over the partner
- space around the apparatus to allow for continuity in sequences

See Figure 5.2 opposite.

The gymnastics curriculum can be constrained by the limitations imposed by the apparatus provided. However, a well-equipped school for gymnastics might include:

- a hinged frame with attachments
- ropes
- trestles with pole
- a two-section bar box (with platform top-to-bottom section)
- a high movement table
- a low movement table
- a set of three low stools, with padded plank or ladder
- four benches (two short, two longer)
- a three-section foam box
- a foam cuboid and ramp
- a junior springboard (where permitted) – this can be used for balancing on, for teaching rolling, when covered with a mat, and for take-off practice and landing when experienced in jumping and landing
- individual mats
- landing mats
- a mat trolley

Many schools use apparatus symbols and labels, similar to those shown in Figures 5.1 and 5.2, both to mark storage places in the hall and for pupil task cards either for setting up or using apparatus. Such a practice can also help to standardise the names of the pieces of apparatus for all users.

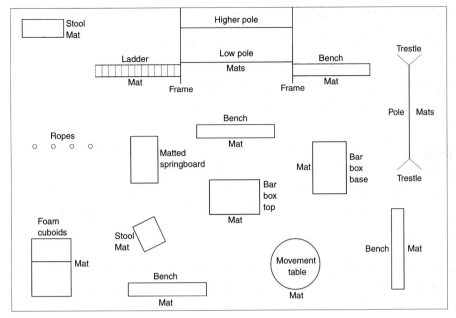

**Figure 5.2** *Apparatus plan for Key Stage 2, Unit 29*

## PLANNING FOR DIFFERENTIATION IN GYMNASTICS

Children bring to their gymnastics a unique blend of physical attributes, including size by way of height, weight and length of limbs, as well as strength, flexibility, power and endurance. They also bring a unique blend of previous experience, a mastery of gross motor skills, a knowledge and understanding of gymnastics and a unique level of intellectual ability and motivation to participate. Add to these the fact that they will almost constantly be changing in relation to one or more of these, and we see the essential requirement to provide a differentiated gymnastics learning experience, so that each child can have an equal opportunity. With this rich baseline also comes the fact that children will progress at different rates in relation to:

- their level of physical development
- their fitness level
- the stage of cognitive, emotional, social and aesthetic development that they have reached
- their attainment in the process of learning motor skills
- their cultural experience
- the level of complexity demonstrated in response to the tasks presented

In planning children's gymnastics learning, there are three opportunities to cater for differentiation:

1 by *provision*, according to the task, by providing a range of challenges offering several alternative activities, with children selecting and tackling the most appropriate

2 by *participation*, where the children's work rate will vary according to their physique, their understanding of the task and its development, and their determination to succeed or to exceed expectations

3 by *outcome*, where the responses to a single practical gymnastics task allow for a range of acceptable performances

By including differentiation in the planning stage, children should expect to be presented with activities that enable them to challenge their previous experience with new learning.

## PLANNING FOR INTEGRATION OF 'TOP GYMNASTICS' AND FOR EXTRA-CURRICULAR GYMNASTICS

With the national concern over poor fitness levels and levels of sport participation and competitive sport achievement by young people, some of the proceeds of the National Lottery are now finding their way into sport provision. The Youth Sport Trust has been set up to provide resources for schools and teachers' courses. The materials produced are intended to supplement, and to be integrated into, the school's gymnastics curriculum. The scheme is called 'Top Gymnastics'. The attractive workcards follow the National Curriculum and provide additional ideas for curriculum planning and content. They are not intended to replace the school's planned curriculum. The Youth Sport Trust has also produced materials for extra-curricular gymnastics, which, along with those available from the British Gymnastics Association, including the Persil Fun Fit Scheme, provide a range of attractive materials and challenges for children of all ages in primary school.

## PLANNING FOR QUALITY TEACHING AND EFFECTIVE LEARNING

Contained in Ofsted's 1996 publication – see the bibliography on page 115 at the end of the book – is a review of the outcomes of Ofsted inspections. This review states that:

'Good practice in the schools visited was characterised by:

- high quality teaching

- high expectations and high levels of achievement
- effective curriculum organisation and planning
- good systems of assessment, recording and reporting'

(Ofsted 1996)

The report goes on to include other characteristics, such as:

- well-qualified staff
- well-planned staff development
- sufficient and appropriate accommodation
- sufficient and appropriate apparatus
- effective co-ordination of the subject
- established routines for dress, behaviour and apparatus handling
- the amount of time devoted by teachers
- a good range and quality of curriculum content and extra-curricular provision
- equality of opportunity and high participation rates
- liaison with other schools and agencies

## CONCLUSION

Does your school match the Ofsted criteria? Do you have a vision for gymnastics teaching and learning? Have you a sound knowledge and understanding of gymnastics and teaching strategies for effective delivery of the curriculum? Do you challenge low expectations and low aspirations in pupils by creating a sense of purpose and achievement? Can your pupils use their gymnastics education as a vehicle for gaining access to other learning, as well as for engaging in gymnastics for its own sake? Is there a climate for success in your school, in which the children increasingly take responsibility for their learning? Are they able to plan, perform and evaluate their own work and to work co-operatively with others? Are they able to analyse and give feedback to others, and do they leave your school as competent and confident gymnasts? Providing a gymnastics curriculum that is challenging, accessible, attainable, progressive and fulfilling for each pupil is the task for the school.

Through gymnastics, children should expect to study and acquire a movement vocabulary that is articulate, skilful and creative, to achieve quality performance and to participate actively and safely. They should develop co-ordination, poise and confidence, and should be able to show precision and fluency, in their movement. Additionally, the teacher's aim for each child should be to produce learners who are physically educated, who maintain a positive self-image in their physical education and who are eager to develop their knowledge, skills and understanding of the subject after they leave primary school. Success for the teacher of young children can also be seen in the longer term when the foundations they laid for their pupils' enduring commitment to physical activity and the maintenance of a healthy lifestyle are brought to fruition.

The purpose of this book is to make a contribution towards the achievement of these aspirations.

# Appendix I
# References and
# further reading

British Amateur Gymnastic Association (BAGA) (1995) *Persil Fun Fit*, BAGA. (Now called the British Gymnastics Association and based at Lilleshall National Sports Centre, near Newport, Shropshire).

British Association of Advisers and Lecturers of Physical Education (BAALPE) (1995) *Safe Practice in Physical Education*, Dudley: Dudley LEA.

Benn, T. and Benn, B. (1992) *Primary Gymnastics*, Cambridge: Cambridge University Press.

Blake, B. Use of Language within the National Curriculum for Physical Education. BAALPE (1996) vol. 32 no. 3.

Department for Education (DFE) (1995) *Physical Education in the National Curriculum*, London: HMSO. (Renamed the Department for Education and Employment in 1996.)

Gallahue, D. and Ozman, J. (1995) *Understanding Motor Development*, 3rd edn, London: W.C. Brown.

Maude, P. (1994) *The Gym Kit* (video and handbook), Albion Television, The Health Promotion Research Trust and Homerton College, Cambridge.

Ofsted (1996) *Physical Education and Sport in Schools – a Survey of Good Practice*, London: HMSO.

PEA (1995) *Teaching Physical Education at Key Stages 1 and 2*, London: Physical Education Association.

The School Curriculum and Assessment Authority (SCAA) (1996) *Physical Education – Consistency in Teacher Assessment, Exemplification of Standards, Key Stage 3* (video and handbook), London: SCAA.

SCAA (1995) *Planning the Curriculum at Key Stages 1 and 2*, London: SCAA.

SCAA (1996) *Nursery Education: Desirable Outcomes for Children's Learning on Entering Compulsory Education*, London: SCAA.

Youth Sport Trust (1997) *Top Gymnastics*. Loughborough: Youth Sport Trust.

# Appendix II
# Year and age groupings for Key Stages 1 and 2

| Reception | 4–5 years | | |
|-----------|-----------|---|---|
| Year 1 | 5–6 | } Infants | } Key Stage 1 |
| Year 2 | 6–7 | | |
| Year 3 | 7–8 | } Lower Juniors | } Key Stage 2 |
| Year 4 | 8–9 | | |
| Year 5 | 9–10 | } Upper Juniors | |
| Year 6 | 10–11 | | |

# Appendix III
# Charts for teachers to use

|  | Balancing | Jumping | Inverting |
|---|---|---|---|
| Small<br>Flexed<br>Tucked |  |  |  |
| Straight<br>Long<br>Extended |  |  |  |
| Wide<br>Star |  |  |  |

Draw or list your work in the boxes

**Figure A.1** *A chart for recording body shapes*

| Action | Technique | Development |
|---|---|---|
| Jump and land | | |
| Travel on feet | | |
| Travel on hands and feet | | |
| Roll | | |
| Balance | | |
| Turn | | |
| Hang | | |
| Swing | | |
| Climb | | |

**Figure A.2** *An analysis and self-assessment chart for basic actions in gymnastics*

| | Travel on feet | Travel on hands and feet | Jump and land | Roll | Balance | Turn | Pull | Push | Hang | Swing | Climb |
|---|---|---|---|---|---|---|---|---|---|---|---|
| Extended long | | | | | | | | | | | |
| Extended wide | | | | | | | | | | | |
| Flexed | | | | | | | | | | | |
| Symmetry | | | | | | | | | | | |
| Asymmetry | | | | | | | | | | | |
| Forwards | | | | | | | | | | | |
| Backwards | | | | | | | | | | | |
| Sideways left | | | | | | | | | | | |
| Sideways right | | | | | | | | | | | |
| Straight | | | | | | | | | | | |
| Curved | | | | | | | | | | | |
| Zig-zag | | | | | | | | | | | |
| High/up | | | | | | | | | | | |
| Medium | | | | | | | | | | | |
| Low/down | | | | | | | | | | | |
| Slowly | | | | | | | | | | | |
| Quickly | | | | | | | | | | | |
| Accelerating | | | | | | | | | | | |
| Decelerating | | | | | | | | | | | |
| Pause | | | | | | | | | | | |
| Rhythm | | | | | | | | | | | |
| Right way up | | | | | | | | | | | |
| Upside-down | | | | | | | | | | | |

**Figure A.3** *Gymnastics vocabulary for building sequences and developing movement memory*

| | SET 1 Ropes | SET 2 Bar box | SET 3 Bench | SET 4 Frame |
|---|---|---|---|---|
| | SET 5 Stools Plank | SET 6 Cuboid and ramp | SET 7 Mat on springboard | SET 8 Tables |

List below actions which extend available apparatus vocabulary:

1 _____
2 _____
3 _____
4 _____
5 _____

6 _____
7 _____
8 _____
9 _____
10 _____

**Figure A.4** *An audit of the apparatus vocabulary of the class, with a list of actions which extend this vocabulary*

All charts: © Patricia Maude, from *Hodder Primary PE: gymnastics*, Hodder & Stoughton, 1997.

# Index